Critical Studies of the Asia-Pacific

Series Editor: **Mark Beeson**, Professor of International Politics, Murdoch University, Australia

Critical Studies of the Asia-Pacific showcases new research and scholarship on what is arguably the most important region in the world in the twenty-first century. The rise of China and the continuing strategic importance of this dynamic economic area to the United States mean that the Asia Pacific will remain crucially important to policy-makers and scholars alike. The unifying theme of the series is a desire to publish the best theoretically informed, original research on the region. Titles in the series cover the politics, economics and security of the region, as well as focussing on its institutional processes, individual countries, issues and leaders.

Titles include:
Stephen Aris
EURASIAN REGIONALISM
The Shanghai Cooperation Organisation

Thomas Birtchnell
INDOVATION
Innovation and a Global Knowledge Economy in India

Toby Carroll
DELUSIONS OF DEVELOPMENT
The World Bank and the Post-Washington Consensus in Southeast Asia

Aurel Croissant and Marco Bünte (*editors*)
THE CRISIS OF DEMOCRATIC GOVERNANCE IN SOUTHEAST ASIA

Aurel Croissant, David Kuehn, Philip Lorenz and Paul W. Chambers
DEMOCRATIZATION AND CIVILIAN CONTROL IN ASIA

Kelly Gerard
ASEAN's ENGAGEMENT OF CIVIL SOCIETY
Regulating Dissent

Shahar Hameiri
REGULATING STATEHOOD
State Building and the Transformation of the Global Order

Felix Heiduk (*editor*)
SECURITY SECTOR REFORM IN SOUTHEAST ASIA
From Policy to Practice

Brendan Howe
THE PROTECTION AND PROMOTION OF HUMAN SECURITY IN EAST ASIA

Jane Hutchison, Wil Hout, Caroline Hughes and Richard Robison
POLITICAL ECONOMY OF THE AID INDUSTRY IN ASIA

Lee Jones
ASEAN, SOVEREIGNTY AND INTERVENTION IN SOUTHEAST ASIA

Jikon Lai
FINANCIAL CRISIS AND INSTITUTIONAL CHANGE IN EAST ASIA

Arndt Michael
INDIA'S FOREIGN POLICY AND REGIONAL MULTILATERALISM

Joel Rathus
JAPAN, CHINA AND NETWORKED REGIONALISM IN EAST ASIA

Claudia Tazreiter and Siew Yean Tham (*editors*)
GLOBALIZATION AND SOCIAL TRANSFORMATION IN THE ASIA-PACIFIC
The Australian and Malayasian Experience

Sow Keat Tok
MANAGING CHINA'S SOVEREIGNTY IN HONG KONG AND TAIWAN

William Tow and Rikki Kersten (*editors*)
BILATERAL PERSPECTIVES ON REGIONAL SECURITY
Australia, Japan and the Asia-Pacific Region

Barry Wain
MALAYSIAN MAVERICK
Mahathir Mohamad in Turbulent Times

Mikael Weissmann
THE EAST ASIAN PEACE
Conflict Prevention and Informal Peacebuilding

Robert G. Wirsing, Christopher Jasparro and Daniel C. Stoll
INTERNATIONAL CONFLICT OVER WATER RESOURCES IN HIMALAYAN ASIA

Critical Studies of the Asia Pacific Series
Series Standing Order ISBN 978–0–230–22896–2 (Hardback)
978–0–230–22897–9 (Paperback)
(*outside North America only*)

You can receive future titles in this series as they are published by placing a standing order. Please contact your bookseller or, in case of difficulty, write to us at the address below with your name and address, the title of the series and the ISBNs quoted above.

Customer Services Department, Macmillan Distribution Ltd, Houndmills, Basingstoke, Hampshire RG21 6XS, England

---

Previous books by authors

Rodan, G. and Hughes, C. *The Politics of Social Accountability in Southeast Asia* (Oxford: Oxford University Press, 2014).

Hout, W. (ed.) *EU Strategies on Governance Reform: Between Development and State-building* (London: Routledge, 2013).

Robison, R. (ed.) *Routledge Handbook of Southeast Asia Politics* (London and New York: Routledge, 2012).

Hout, W. and Robison, R. (eds) *Governance and the Depoliticisation of Development* (London: Routledge, 2009).

Hughes, C. *Dependent Communities: Aid and Politics in Cambodia and Timor-Leste* (Ithaca: Cornell South East Asia Program Publications, 2009).

Hout, W. *The Politics of Aid Selectivity: Good Governance Criteria in U.S., World Bank and Dutch Foreign Assistance* (London: Routledge, 2007).

Hewison, K. and Robison, R. *East Asia and the Trials of Neo-Liberalism* (London: Routledge, 2006).

Robison, R. and Hadiz, V. *Reorganising Power in Indonesia: The Politics of Oligarchy in an Age of Markets* (London: Routledge, 2004).

Political Economy and the Aid Industry in Asia

Jane Hutchison
Murdoch University, Australia

Wil Hout
Erasmus University Rotterdam, The Netherlands

Caroline Hughes
University of Bradford, UK

and

Richard Robison
Murdoch University, Australia

First published 2014 by
PALGRAVE MACMILLAN

Palgrave Macmillan in the UK is an imprint of Macmillan Publishers Limited, registered in England, company number 785998, of Houndmills, Basingstoke, Hampshire RG21 6XS.

Palgrave Macmillan in the US is a division of St Martin's Press LLC, 175 Fifth Avenue, New York, NY10010.

Palgrave Macmillan is the global academic imprint of the above companies and has companies and representatives throughout the world.

Palgrave® and Macmillan® are registered trademarks in the United States, the United Kingdom, Europe and other countries.

ISBN 978–1–137–30360–8

This book is printed on paper suitable for recycling and made from fully managed and sustained forest sources. Logging, pulping and manufacturing processes are expected to conform to the environmental regulations of the country of origin.

A catalogue record for this book is available from the British Library.

A catalog record for this book is available from the Library of Congress.

Typeset by MPS Limited, Chennai, India.

Contents

List of Tables

Acknowledgements

The study has its origins in a project funded by AusAID under the Australian Development Research Awards Program and commenced in 2009. For some of the early findings, see, *The Elephant in the Room: Politics and the Development Problem*, Policy Monograph, 13–14 December, 2010, Asia Research Centre, Murdoch University. Chapter 2 has drawn on parts of the chapter by Richard Robison, 'Strange Bedfellows: Political Alliances in the Making of Neo-Liberal Governance', in Wil Hout and Richard Robison (eds) *Governance and the Depoliticisation of Development* (London: Routledge, 2009): 15–28. Parts of Chapter 3 were published as an article by Wil Hout in *Third World Quarterly*, vol. 33, no. 3 (2012), pp. 429–46 under the title 'The Anti-politics of Development: Donor Agencies and the Political Economy of Governance'. Chapters 5, 6 and 7 have used parts of the article 'Development Effectiveness and the Politics of Commitment' by Caroline Hughes and Jane Hutchison, published in *Third World Quarterly*, vol. 33, no. 1 (2012), pp. 17–36. Chapters 5, 6, and 7 also draw on Indonesian cases studies from Mohtat Mas'oed, J. Nicolaas Warouw and Aris Arif Mundayat (Gadja Mada University) and Ian Wilson (Murdoch University). Ian Wilson's case study appears in *The Elephant in the Room: Politics and the Development Problem*. Ingebjørg Helland Scarpello provided editorial assistance, with funds from the Asia Research Centre.

List of Abbreviations

ADB	Asian Development Bank
AJI	*Aliansi Jurnalis Independen* (the Alliance of Independent Journalists (Indonesia))
AusAID	Australian Agency for International Development
BaPPEDA	*Badan Perencana Pembangunan Daerah* (Regional Development Planning Agency)
CMP	Community Mortgage Programme
CoCSOaC	Coalition of Civil Society Organisations Against Corruption
CPIA	Country Policy and Institutional Assessment
CPP	Cambodian People's Party
CSO	Civil Society Organisation
DEK	Department for Effectiveness and Quality
DFGG	Demand for Good Governance
DFID	Department for International Development
DGIS	Directorate-General for International Cooperation
DLP	Developmental Leadership Program
DMH	Human Rights, Good Governance and Humanitarian Aid
DMV	Department of Human Rights and Peacebuilding
EU	European Union
FAKTA	Jakarta Residents Forum
GSDRC	Governance and Social Development Resource Centre
HUDCC	Housing Urban Development Coordinating Council
IDA	International Development Association
IDS	Institute of Development Studies
IMF	International Monetary Fund

KKN	*korupsi, kolusi, dan nepotisme* (corruption, collusion, and nepotism)
MASPs	Multi-annual Strategic Plans
MPBM	*Musyawarah Pembangunan Bermitra Masyarakat* (Community Partnerships Development Forum)
Musrenbang	*Musyawarah Perencanaan Pembangunan* (Community Consultation on Development Planning)
NGOs	Non-governmental organisations
NSAs	Non-State Actors
ODI	Overseas Development Institute
OECD	Organisation for Economic Co-operation and Development
PCAs	Power and Change Analysis
PNPM	*Program Nasional Pemberdayaan Masyarakat* (National Program on Community Empowerment)
PREM	Poverty Reduction and Economic Management
PRS	Poverty Reduction Strategies
PRSPs	Poverty Reduction Strategy Papers
Satpol PP	*Satuan Polisi Pamong Praja* (Civil Service Police Unit)
SGACA	Strategic Governance and Corruption Analysis
SIDA	Swedish International Development Cooperation Agency
TPP	Trans-Pacific Partnership
TRT	Thai Rak Thai
UDHA	Urban Development and Housing Act
UN	United Nations
UNDP	United Nations Development Programme
USAID	US Agency for International Development
WTO	World Trade Organisation

1
Introduction

Our argument

This book examines attempts made by policy-makers in development agencies and banks to understand how political economy shapes the way development programmes take root in developing countries and how it has defined their outcomes. It also seeks to explain why it had proven difficult to establish more recent ideas about political economy, such as the Drivers of Change approach and its outliers and successors, as the basis for new models of development practice and strategies for development effectiveness. Finally, the book proposes a different way of applying political economy approaches – on the basis of what we are calling 'structural political economy' – to development policies and aid programming.

It is central to our thesis that development approaches are not divided between those that reject the importance of political economy and those who accept it. Rather, we propose, development agendas have always embraced a concrete idea of political economy and recognised how its dynamics present particular challenges for policy-makers. An important difference is how some traditions of development theory believe political obstacles can be overcome by technical and policy fixes, including market reforms and the transplant of certain institutions and forms of governance, while others believe that development strategies require direct engagement within the political process to mobilise or neutralise contending political and social interests.

The primary aim of the book is to explain the nature of different ideas and ideologies of political economy and how these have shaped particular models of development thinking and more practical strategies and approaches. More specifically, we intend to focus on the way many of the unintended outcomes and counter-productive consequences of development efforts over the years have their roots in particular (and misconceived) understandings of political economy.

Approaches to political economy

At a broad level, we have identified two main approaches to political economy that have dominated the development industry since the rise of the market models of social and economic change took root in the World Bank in the 1980s (see Toye, 1987). One can be more generally categorised as rational choice or public choice political economy and has been ascendant in the World Bank, and most development agencies and the financial ministries of most Western developed economies, particularly the US, Britain and Australia. It is a model that normatively aims at establishing market values and principles, as the basis not only for economic behaviour but for the way political authority and social life more broadly, including the practices of governance and citizenship, are constructed.

Yet, we propose that the central political problem embedded within this political economy approach is why developing economies (in this case) nowhere seem to replicate a world defined by the voluntary exchanges of rational, utility-maximising individuals. In the view of public choice theorists this is because individuals can form coalitions to make predatory raids on the public interest to secure their vested interests rather than to solve collective action dilemmas (see Bates, 1981; Olson, 1982). The task, therefore, has been understood as one that seeks to impose the public welfare, understood in the terms of market rationality, over these self-seeking interests. There are numerous recipes for achieving this goal.

Perhaps the predominant approach has been that championed by the World Bank, aimed at insulating markets from the contending rationality of politics and constructing a technocratic form of authority that could rise above vested interests. Subsequently, we have seen more populist strategies aimed at bypassing the predatory interests that form within and around the governments of developing economies and which seek to directly mobilise civil society behind the market agenda. These approaches attempt to strengthen 'social capital' and, thus, the capacity of grass-roots organisations to support the market agenda (see Harriss, 2001). This has been the political strategy that underpins the World Bank's Poverty Reduction Strategies (PRSs).

Other attempts have been to move beyond the understanding of political economy as a contest between rationality and vested interest towards a more complex appreciation of the configurations of power and interest within which development agendas are contested. More than this, it is proposed that development policy and practice must engage directly in the political process to improve aid effectiveness, supporting progressive elements that can be champions of development in addressing collective action problems.[1]

Political economy and development policy

In this book we explain how these understandings of political economy have become embedded in specific development outcomes that can not only deepen problems of poverty and inequity but also contradict many of the very normative objectives of market-based ideas of governance and social order. We necessarily start out from a very different, structural idea of political economy and how it shapes the dynamics of developing economies. A central feature of this idea is that political economy is defined within the terms of certain relationships of power that bind society together and by the asymmetries of economic and political resources that are embedded in these relationships.

In this view, it is difficult to propose technocratic forms of governance that are abstracted from the real struggles between different interests. And it is difficult to simply neutralise so-called 'predatory' interests or to mobilise perceived progressive forces and 'champions of development' behind specific policy agendas. These cannot be easily detached from the broader set of power relationships that define society and from their dependence upon the structures within which wealth, jobs and security are organised and allocated. In other words, they are anchored within the existing social order. A second point is that, by definition, the most powerful forces tend to be content with the status quo, including the reality of poverty and the pervasiveness of 'bad governance', while progressives or discontents are invariably politically weaker and less able to influence the course of events.

At the same time we have been drawn into the related question of why some ideas about political economy are more enthusiastically embraced by development organisations than others. This is the political economy of development organisations. Development agencies understandably operate within larger geo-political and economic priorities of donor countries. Policies designed to favour perceived 'progressive' interests, or that propose to enhance the power of poor people, bring both political risks and administrative difficulties for donors.

And development agencies must demonstrate to their funders, usually governments, that they are efficient and responsible in the use of public money. Hence, there is pressure to favour ways of doing things that are able to be reported in quantifiable terms. The effective disbursements of funds can fit more easily into the technocratic model of development policy. There is an established literature explaining why political economy approaches embodied in the Drivers of Change thesis have not been taken up in a systematic way within agencies such as Department for International Development (DFID) and why the technocratic model continues to prevail (e.g., Unsworth, 2009).

Our own discussions with senior officials in the Australian Agency for International Development (AusAID) substantiate these points. Officials have made it clear that policy is constrained by risk conceived within larger national economic and political priorities set by the Australian government. They stressed the career and institutional importance given to proper project design, implementation and reporting in relation to the allocation and spending of very large aid budgets. It is the latter task of reporting that occupies officials on the ground. Also, the sensitivities of talking in more political terms to project and programme counterparts are stressed. These are understandable objectives and concerns. Nevertheless, they inhibit the incorporation of political economy insights where these threaten to disturb particular political or social orders that may be useful to donor governments or international investors, or where they require programmes that involve longer term and more intense presence on the ground and there is less capacity to move large budgets quickly.

If such difficulties apply to strategies aimed at enhancing 'drivers of change' then they apply in greater measure to the prospects for an approach based on a political economy defined by conflicts over power and its distribution. How can such a study shape ideas about development and development policy if it raises questions about the very ideas of political economy and public management that define development organisations? This is a dilemma at the heart of relationships between the intellectual analysis of the development process and the way development policy is constructed.

We see it as less of a problem than is often imagined if we accept that there are two levels of study and research about development problems within research bodies and universities. It is a fact that the bulk of such studies are highly instrumental in their nature. They are aimed at enhancing the efficiency of policies or solving their dilemmas within the existing intellectual paradigms and political economies of development organisations. In other words, they operate as an extension of the development bureaucracies themselves and facilitate their operations: they are concerned with such questions as how to better measure 'good governance' or to report more efficiently the allocation of funds, even to grass-roots organisations and non-governmental organisations (NGOs).

Another sort of study is aimed at stretching the existing intellectual boundaries and the political economies of development organisations themselves and of the policy-makers within these bureaucracies. Like the Drivers of Change thesis they have little prospect of broad integration into policy, at least in existing circumstances. But does this mean that such studies should not be undertaken? Here, we make the following points. One is that the study of development and development policy should not be limited by the extent to which it is immediately translatable into existing policy frameworks or acceptable within the political economies of development agencies. Such reservoirs of knowledge can be rapidly made redundant as circumstances change within donor governments and in developing countries themselves.

The second point is that we must assume that at least some officials in donor agencies are not simply process-driven bureaucrats for whom any department is the same as any other. We must assume there is an interest in and knowledge of the substance of the development debate itself, even where the practical constraints on policy-making limit the easy translation of many ideas into action. In other words, that there are people who possess a reservoir of knowledge outside the policy arena that enables strategic engagement with fluid and rapidly changing circumstances.

At the same time, we propose that a sophisticated understanding of political economy can provide better explanations of why some aid programmes go wrong and give policy-makers at least a better capacity to know what not to do and when. For example, the public choice political economy idea proposes that the privatisation of property rights is necessarily and universally productive of increasing economic efficiency, wealth and public welfare. In reality, the dismantling of public and community property rights has often led to concentrations of wealth and power in the hands of narrow oligarchies and the impoverishment of populations. A different sort of political economy, such as that in this study, will enable policy-makers to better understand that the consequences of such policies will not always be the same and to evaluate the likely consequences of allocating private titles and rights over land and property in specific circumstances.

The second immediate policy lesson is that alliances with assumed progressive forces will not necessarily produce progressive policy reforms. Progressive forces will often not possess the power to drive reform. Or they may be easily transformed by cooption. On the contrary it is important that progressive policies may be achieved through tactical alliances, even with conservative interests where they see short-term benefits and where little trust is involved. Of course, engaging in such alliances can be a risky proposition. But the risk can be offset if there is a deep understanding of their political economy.

Thirdly, this book contributes to policy debates about the aid effectiveness agenda. The focus on 'managing for results', introduced in the Paris Declaration on Aid Effectiveness, has clearly cemented donors' focus on results measurement (High-Level Forum on Aid Effectiveness, 2005). Such focus on impact assessment is not necessarily helpful for more progressive development organisations, which are not content with existing power distributions and would prefer to induce social change in highly unequal developing countries (Eyben et al., 2013). Development policies, as indicated by former US Agency for International Development (USAID)'s Administrator, Andrew Natsios (2010), among others, are inherently risky. Yet, the need to 'manage for results' may easily produce risk-averse behaviour on the part of development agencies, as they feel the pressure, for instance from parliaments, to adopt programmes with measurable output, but less transformative value. As aptly phrased by Natsios (2010: 3), the focus on measurement 'ignores a central principle of development theory – that those development programmes that are most precisely and easily measured are the least transformational, and those programmes that are most transformational are the least measurable'. Structural political economy calls for a less risk-averse attitude among donors and more direct engagement to bringing about social and political change.

Structure of the book

The book is divided into two parts. The first part, including Chapters 2–4, looks more intensively at the problems described above. It explores some of the deep paradoxes that define the relationship between different ideas of political economy and the practice of development. It also examines how the political economy of development agencies themselves, including their ideological and administrative practices, also shapes the boundaries of development practice more broadly. The second part of the book, including Chapters 5–7, develops the structural political economy perspective and takes a closer look at the implementation of political economy analysis in the context of specific case studies from Southeast Asia. Chapter 8 contains the conclusions of the study.

In Chapter 2, we look at development strategies and policies that emerge from rational choice ideas of political economy and the attempts to insulate markets from politics, including by means of technocratic forms of political authority and social organisation. Our main purpose here is to explain the central paradox of this approach. We argue that the very forces identified within the rational choice political economy approach as predatory interlopers on the market society are in reality integral elements in the political establishment of market society. Here, we argue that the introduction of market agendas and new forms of governance often requires the political backing of powerful oligarchies that are both illiberal and corrupt in their nature and reinforces their authority. In other words, the powerful interests that are the essential political allies of the market agenda and so essential in politically pushing aside the opponents of markets, whether these are reactionary populists or various forms of social democracy, are themselves the very forces that produce 'bad governance' and obstruct many of the market-based reforms of Western development organisations. We ask how this seemingly contradictory process takes place and whether such predatory interests are the precursors of an inevitable liberal transformation or whether they represent a new model of development outside the assumptions of Western development banks and aid organisations.

Chapter 3 analyses the 'political economy turn' experienced by many development agencies over the last decade. On the basis of their awareness of realities behind the façade of formal institutions in developing countries, donor agencies started to develop tools for political economy assessment, which, they hoped, would inform their decision-making on development projects and programmes. The chapter discusses three examples of political economy assessment: the UK's Drivers of Change, the Dutch Strategic Governance and Corruption Analysis, and the World Bank's approach to the Political Economy of Policy Reform and its Problem-Driven Governance and Political Economy Analysis. Our analysis of the political economy of donors brings us to an explanation of the limited uptake of political economy assessment in the day-to-day practice of development policy.

The fourth chapter holds a discussion of ideas developed by scholars, consultants and practitioners in the aid industry to advance the implementation of political economy insights by donor agencies. We focus on the political economy community that has developed as a result of the recent attention to political economy analysis, and zero in on their assumption that collective action problems are central to development politics. We analyse the mainstream of the community's thinking – specifically the liberal pluralist understandings of political agency, and working politically through developmental leaders and coalitions and/or the manipulation of incentives – in order to position our own structural approach. We argue that our understanding of political economy and its application in contexts of developing countries differs substantially from the mainstream: our view being that a rethinking of the role of institutions and the politics surrounding them is necessary to take account of power relations in the prevailing social order. This implies, we argue, seeing development as a public good and the object of collective action entails a misguided conception of what pro-poor development policies actually involve.

The book's second part utilises structural political economy to analyse the dilemmas of development and aid programming in our Southeast Asian case studies. Chapter 5 explains our understanding of development as a process of contested structural change and, hence, of aid programming as highly constrained interventions in ongoing political struggles, in material and ideological terms. Given the pre-dominant attention to institutions and their reform within market-based political economy models, we especially cover the limitations of this as a development political strategy. In the same chapter, the case studies of four governance reform agendas in three countries – Cambodia, Indonesia and the Philippines – are introduced on the basis of the nature of existing conflicts, the various actors involved, how they understand 'development' and hence their interests in and responses to the proposed reforms.

The sixth chapter presents a typology of reformers and their alliances that incorporates our structural political economy insights. We dif-ferentiate reform actors according to the nature of their commitment to specific aid programmes and, similarly, non-reformers on the basis of the level of their indifference or opposition. Whereas development agencies tend to look to partner with strongly committed, powerful reformers, we reiterate that power-holders are not likely to be dedicated or idealist reformers because their interests lie in the status quo and, conversely, the most dedicated, idealist reformers are generally lacking power, influence or authority because they (or the subordinate groups on whose behalf they may act) are not well served by the prevailing social order. As a result, at best, elites will normally offer only oppor-tunistic support for reform, when they see a benefit coming their way, for example, through greater access to funding and enhanced political legitimacy, or simply to maintain good relations with donor agencies to keep their options open. By the same token, among idealist reform-ers there will be pragmatists who are willing to compromise on reform goals for more than the concrete gains resulting from collaboration with donors. However, there can be political risks in this for ideal-ists in terms of their ongoing relations with constituencies and allies. The implication for donor agencies is that political economy realities require them to devote more time and resources to tactical relation-ships and alliances with a range of state and non-state actors.

In Chapter 7, we pursue this argument through an added analy-sis of alliances. Alliances denote a wider set of relationships in aid programming than does the notion of 'partnership'. We make clear our view that country 'ownership' – of the kind extolled by current international development modalities – is not achievable because of the conflicts of interest, both material and ideological, which development involves and aid programming has to address. Taking ownership seriously requires donor agencies to let go of their singular expectations of 'partnership' in order to be more discerning about the range of possible relationships, given the sorts of actors involved, their conflicts and interests, and levels of commitment and preferred strategies vis-à-vis reform. To illustrate our points, the chapter also cites examples from Southeast Asia. It closes with a discussion of the implications for donor agencies.

   Chapter 8 is the conclusion in which the focus and main arguments of the book are restated. We cover the key political economy constraints facing the aid industry today: those within donor agencies themselves and in recipient countries, as well as the political economy of policy compromise and of the changing global environment for aid. Donor agencies are on the road to nowhere in terms of aid effectiveness if they do not go beyond a rhetorical commitment to working politically. The road to somewhere, we can only repeat, lies in grasping the difficult realities of development politics and proceeding on the basis of the insights from structural political economy.

Part I
Development Agencies
and the Reality of Politics

2
Realities of Political Economy: The Elephant in the Room

Introduction

The idea that the political landscape can be reordered in a technocratic way by means of market reform and institutional change has dominated thinking in the economic ministries and development agencies of the major Western countries since the early 1980s. It has been heavily influenced by the rational choice/public choice view of politics as a world of self-serving behaviour where vested interests accumulate wealth by mobilising political power and influence to undermine the market mechanism. This neoliberal view initially assumed that the imposition of markets and the ending of government intervention in the economy would be enough in themselves to neutralise the predatory raids on the state that defined the rent-seeking society. As this expectation evaporated, development strategy was switched from an emphasis on rolling out markets to that of building strong institutions to enforce the rule of markets, to insulate markets from the 'irrationalities' of politics and to provide incentives for market-oriented behaviour. In essence, neoliberals sought to replace politics, as they saw it, with technocratic and managerial forms of authority and 'good governance' based on market principles and values.

This approach sits uncomfortably with a second, partially overlapping, stream of thought that is derived from the pluralist and more classical liberal understanding of society and politics, where civil society is conceived as an inherently progressive arena of self-reliant individuals (in reality the middle class). The political task, in this view, moves from one of insulating a technocratic form of authority

13

from the demands of the populace to that of mobilising progressive social forces behind liberal development objectives and to that of incorporating society into markets (see Chapter 4). How this objective will be achieved is defined by the way the seemingly inherent weakness of civil society is understood. Within the neoliberal view, predominant within the World Bank and in the poverty alleviation debates, the problem is defined by a lack of capacity in society and an absence of cohesion and networks able to support market agendas. This requires a highly technocratic project to construct social capital and to establish new ideas of citizenship based on the market (see Jayasuriya, 2006; Carroll, 2009; Hatcher, 2009).

As we shall also see in later chapters, both the attempts to construct a technocratic form of public authority insulated from the rationality of politics as well as attempts to bypass politics by means of popular ownership of development programmes, involving participation, partnership and inclusion, negotiation and leadership by 'champions of development' have confronted fundamental difficulties. These difficulties, we propose, have their roots in the way both neoliberals and pluralists understand political economy. Our task in this chapter is to explain the dilemmas faced by these reformers.

In particular, we argue, the development process is not defined in terms of resistance versus transformation but rather as part of larger conflicts among emerging and entrenched interests and forces to shape the new market societies and establish new forms of social and political power and governance within the market system.[1] In this context, institutions and different forms of governance, for example, cease to be merely good or bad in any abstracted sense. Rather, they are the products of certain interests and are integral to a specific social and political order.

It is important that the players in these social orders, including potential progressive forces, cannot be abstracted from the larger relationships of power that bind society together and from the asymmetries of power and wealth that define them. It is difficult, for example, to expect farmers to push for reforms where their actions confront landowners or other interests who control the rents, the credit or the markets on which they rely. Such structural inequalities, we argue, present development organisations with a critical dilemma. Progressive forces, the potential champions of development, by definition, rarely possess the power to drive the sort of reforms that would properly regulate markets or provide rule of law. On the other hand, the interests of those with the power to drive reforms prefer forms of governance that preserve their own political authority within the new markets society.

And there is an important paradox in this process. The very forms of social power and political authority created and consolidated within the new market economies can also become the central obstacle to the agendas of development banks and the development agencies of donor countries, particularly in regard to ideas about governance and democracy. This chapter develops, in particular, the following three main points.

First, the spread of the market economy has enabled the emergence and concentration of particular forms of political and economic power and authority. In the early years of market capitalism complex oligarchies are often the beneficiaries of this process. These emerge within the broad rules of markets as the beneficiaries of privatisation and market deregulation and as public or communal property rights are transferred into private hands. They adopt techno-managerial prescriptions for political rule as a means of denying the legitimacy of popular interests (Robison, 1986; Jesudason, 1996; Jayasuriya and Rodan, 2007). They are also often the beneficiaries of globalised economic relationships, gaining access to international financial and capital markets and being able to circulate and insulate their wealth within these markets (Moore, 2001). These forms of oligarchy are at once integral to the neoliberal project and a primary source of what neoliberals understand as 'bad governance'. They are the forces development organisations must deal with and constitute the primary elephant in the room for neoliberal policymakers.

The second point is that these new market-based oligarchies or regimes are far from being transitory or dysfunctional. Even where they confront economic crisis and political collapse, such entrenched interests are prepared to resist serious institutional reform as these may threaten their political ascendancy (Bardhan, 1989). Where they may seem inefficient or dysfunctional in achieving economic growth or establishing orderly authority they derive resilience from their ability to deliver power and wealth to key interests in society and in this sense they are highly functional and coherent (Chabal and Daloz, 1999). Attempting to remove or bypass such oligarchies, whether by means of institutional engineering or the cultivation of 'progressive' forces

in society, fails to understand that such oligarchies and their beneficiaries constitute nothing less than a social order defined by dense
networks of power relationships and hierarchies of authority.

At the same time – and this is the third point made in this chapter – it
must be realised that such oligarchies enjoy ambiguous relations with
donor governments. They provide the political muscle to sweep away
the opponents of market capitalism, whether these are the remnants
of state capitalist regimes, middle-class liberals or radical or reactionary populist movements. They can protect markets from certain
forms of politics and liberate powerful private interests from a range
of collective social demands in relation to taxation, social welfare,
environmental protection or labour rights. These contradictory relationships mean that development agencies and technocratic market
reformers can come into conflict with international investors and the
foreign ministries within the donor countries themselves over the
priorities of 'good governance' or the importance of progressive forces
in the reform process.

The aim of this chapter is, first, to explain how the major development banks and organisations have attempted to protect markets
from what they see as the predatory raids of rent-seeking coalitions
and why institutions and ideas of 'good governance' are central to
their strategies. Second is to explain why these strategies have largely
failed and to draw out the essential political paradox where the spread
of the market economy consolidates the entrenchment of illiberal
social and political authority: the elephant in the room for donor
countries.

From the roll-out of markets to containing political risks

As we have previously noted, the major development banks and
organisations have been dominated by a public choice (neoliberal)
understanding of political economy based on a view of a society
defined by the voluntary transactions of rational, utility-maximising
individuals. In this view, the main challenge to the establishment of
market economies is the resolution of collective action dilemmas posed
by self-serving behaviour. Throughout the 1970s and 1980s it had been
generally assumed that the advance of the market would be enough in
itself to end problems of corruption and arbitrary rule in developing
countries by removing the basis of rent-seeking by the state (for an

overview see Toye, 1987: 47–70). Also, it was thought few institutional prerequisites would be needed beyond some basic property rights in the initial stages of market transformation. This view was an important justification for strategies of 'shock therapy' in Russia and Eastern Europe (see Sachs, 1992; Rapaczynski, 1996).

However, the 1997–98 Asian Financial Crisis gave rise to increasing scepticism of the self-regulating capacities of markets within the neoliberal camp itself. Neoliberal agendas for global economic change and development gradually shifted from a simple plan to roll out markets through policy reform to a new concern for containing the risks that seem invariably to accompany their rise. It was increasingly accepted that markets needed strong institutions and good governance. As early as the 1980s, in the so-called Berg Report, advocates within the World Bank argued that the growing crisis of development in sub-Saharan Africa, with its pervasive corruption and client-based politics, could only be addressed by the construction of institutions able to ensure the effective regulation of the market (World Bank, 1981).

The problem was: where would these institutions come from? It was initially assumed these would emerge seamlessly as rational individuals dealt in an instrumentally rational manner with new collective problems of transaction costs and information asymmetries that accompanied markets (North, 1984; Williamson, 1987). However, as some public choice political economists observed, it was entirely rational for coalitions to organise collectively for the purposes of making predatory raids on the state rather than to establish the collective goods that make markets work (Buchanan and Tullock, 1962; Bates, 1981; Olson, 1982). This seeming dilemma led some theorists to argue that only the state could provide the institutions that would address collective action dilemmas, even though these would necessarily reflect interests rather than an abstracted need for efficiency (North, 1995: 20). This line of thinking made its way into policy thinking in the World Bank (see World Bank, 1997). Yet, where the liberal pluralist idea of the benign state had been replaced with the public choice idea of a state that is necessarily predatory and whose politicians and officials deal in the currency of rents and privileges it became difficult to explain how the state would drive the reform process. As Gamble (2006) has stated it, neoliberals had arrived at a point where neither state nor society could be trusted. It seemed that there was nowhere to go.

Within the neoliberal camp, it became increasingly accepted that only enlightened technocrats operating above the demands of politics could protect the general welfare of society against the self-serving behaviour of vested interests (cf. Grindle, 1991; Williamson, 1994). Indeed, technocratic elites, often dominating key economic and financial ministries and agencies in developing economies, were to be key allies for reformers within the main development agencies of the West. These were to play an important role in designing and implementing market neoliberal reform agendas, including the agendas of the so-called Washington Consensus, involving market deregulation, privatisation and monetary control. For example, Chile's famous 'Los Chicago Boys' in the 1970s had their equivalents in the so-called 'Berkeley Mafia' who, almost a decade earlier, had begun to play a central policy role in Soeharto's Indonesia. In Russia, technocrats like Anatoly Chubais wielded enormous authority over policy during the Yeltsin period of the early 1990s while in Zambia, the ubiquitous Harvard Institute for International Development and the so-called 'Harvard Boys' in the early 1990s were similarly influential.

Yet, despite the flow of hundreds of millions of dollars into programmes of institutional reform, including new constitutional rules and regulatory processes, problems of inefficient public sectors, corruption, arbitrary authority and opaque regulation of markets have continued to proliferate and deepen across developing economies. Within the World Bank and other mainline development agencies these were initially explained as problems of design or sequencing, requiring more precise recalibration of the way incentives are structured within the new institutional arrangements to produce specific behavioural changes (see World Bank, 2002a: 16–60; Rosser, 2009). Above all, something was needed to ensure that policy and institutions worked for markets. This was the genesis of the 'good governance' agenda that now moved to centre stage within the development agencies and banks of the West.

Neoliberals have understood 'good governance' as a mechanism to provide efficient public and private management for markets. As the World Bank (2002a: 99) has stated it: '[t]he ability of the state to provide institutions that make markets more efficient is sometimes referred to as good governance'. Thus, 'good governance' ensures efficiency in public administration, rule of law and regulation of corporate life, including competition laws and anti-corruption watchdogs, arms-length procurement processes and the outsourcing of public services and supply. But the idea of governance has spilled over into wider agendas for regulation and authority at the political and social level. It offers a technological and managerial model of authority designed to insulate markets form the contending rationality of politics, with its assumed predatory tendencies. As economist Hal Hill (2000: 4) observed in his analysis of Indonesia after the Asian Financial Crisis: 'One of the big challenges of the coming years will be to find a way of separating the economic and commercial world from the political world'.

Broadly understood as a form of authority defined by market principles that could be translated into legal or constitutional rules (Gill, 1995), the idea of governance enables a vast range of problems related to economic efficiency and political order and legitimacy to be approached without any reference to the contentious arenas of power and politics (Hewitt de Alcántara, 1998). More practically, the idea of good governance can be used to bypass opponents (vested interests) through modes of technocratic and managerial rule. In the words of one of the main World Bank reports on the topic (2002a: 99), 'good governance requires the power to carry out policies and develop institutions that may be unpopular among some – or even a majority – of the population'.

This explains the mixture of admiration and disapproval with which Singapore is regarded. As Rodan (2006b: 202) points out, Singapore regularly appears at the top of tables of economic freedom produced by various market-oriented foundations and by the *Wall Street Journal*. Singapore clearly illustrates the attractions of government that can guarantee to private investors high levels of political stability and administrative predictability while also containing demands from distributional coalitions where these run counter to technocratic priorities of efficiency and growth.

As we shall see, such views also feed into a deep ambivalence about democracy within the neoliberal camp where it is regarded as a mechanism that potentially unleashes distributional coalitions.[2] By redefining the relationship between state and society within *de facto* social contracts, technocratic governance can free market-elites from the debilitating effects of bargaining with political parties and trade unions. At the same time, such ideas as participation and citizenship can be reformulated in terms of functional co-option into market society rather than in terms of collective rights to contest political agendas embodied in classical liberal or social democratic thinking (Jayasuriya, 2005: 33–6). And by regarding poverty as a problem of capacity rather than one of highly unequal power relationships the threat of redistribution of power and wealth can be avoided.

The immediate task here is to explain how these attempts to create new market states and societies have been undermined, not by the opponents of markets – including economic nationalists, socialists, or by liberals or local populists – but by the very forces and interests that are the products of markets who provide the political muscle for the broader market agenda.

How the 'sorcerer's apprentices' expropriated the market

Despite the prominence of technocrats in the economic ministries of many developing economies, these have generally not possessed a substantial power base of their own. This fact has limited their ability to act autonomously of the political and bureaucratic forces that dominated the state and their allies within business and more broadly among the propertied classes of society. These political coalitions have often seen markets as a means of accumulating new sources of private wealth and building new forms of political authority rather than as instruments to achieve greater efficiency in the allocation of economic resources and the pursuit of economic growth.

The privatisation of large state monopolies and companies has frequently become a mechanism for oligarchies to expropriate public resources and state corporate wealth. Property rights have enabled new political entrepreneurs to claim state assets or private possession of community land where title to these was not clear. And the embrace of globalisation has had ambiguous results. Opening economies to global markets has meant that new private interests can now access flows of finance from international lenders and investors who are willing to accept the risks of highly politicised markets and arbitrary systems of regulation. As we shall see, neoliberal models of techno-managerial authority have also offered various illiberal regimes a new means of legitimising authoritarian rule in the name of economic efficiency and the need to protect markets from the excesses of representative politics. In other words, those who had politically cleared the way for neoliberal market reform and who had become its beneficiaries were also to become the primary obstacles to reforms in governance.

Such a seemingly paradoxical confluence of markets, market values and institutions with various forms of oligarchy and illiberal state authority has been a common feature of the early period of market transformation throughout the developing world. Nowhere has this process been starker than in sub-Saharan Africa where it had become clear, after just a decade of intensive structural adjustment and investment by the World Bank and other agencies, that economic stagnation and political crisis had become endemic (van de Walle, 2001). Market reforms had accompanied the consolidation of predatory forms of politics and the concentration of economic power and wealth in the hands of politicians. These used their political authority to dispense patronage, monopolies and contracts within networks of clients. No powerful, independent bourgeoisie emerged in these circumstances (see Leys, 1996: 164–87). As mentioned earlier, it was in relation to the African experience that the World Bank began to express doubts that deregulation of markets and privatisation was enough in itself to address problems of poverty and predatory behaviour.

While Africa has been considered a special case by many analysts, a place where chaotic and incoherent states ruled over disorganised and fractured bourgeoisie, market reforms also provided the circumstances for the consolidation of oligarchies in quite different situations, including where state power was extensive, organised and cohesive. Perhaps the most dramatic illustration of this took place following the IMF inspired programmes of 'shock therapy' that transformed the economics and ultimately the politics of post-Soviet Russia in the early 1990. Here, the Yeltsin government provided newly influential technocrats, including Yegor Gaidar and Anatoly Chubais, with the authority to direct a programme of radical market reforms that saw vast swathes of the state sector pass into private hands almost overnight. As state assets were swapped for loans, a system of opportunistic private oligarchy emerged to be governed, initially at least, by violence and murder presided over by gangsters and mediated within a highly corrupt state bureaucracy (see Silverman and Yanowitch, 1997; Volkov, 2002; Oversloot, 2006).

In the Middle East as well, nationalist and state capitalist authoritarian regimes gave way, in the 1970s and 1980s to more globalised and market-based forms of despotism with the rise of Sadat and Mubarak

in Egypt and Benjedid in Algeria, among others. As these economies were opened to global markets, private business interests were
established and consolidated under the umbrella of the state, often
embracing the families of political power-holders and senior bureaucrat
(see Colas, 2004; King, 2007).

This general pattern was also prevalent in Southeast Asia. Vigorous
enforcement of structural adjustment reform in the Philippines by
the World Bank in the 1980s and 1990s consolidated the ascendancy
of old political and economic elites in the import and export sectors
but did not tackle the practices of monopoly and political favour that
sustained this rise (Bello et al., 1982; Hawes, 1987; Hutchison, 1997).
In Thailand, the rise of private business as a political power instrument was made possible as deregulated global and domestic financial
and banking systems and equity markets in the 1980s and 1990s
paved the way for a new raft of individuals to consolidate themselves
outside the big Sino-Thai banks in finance, property and telecommu-
nications (Lauridsen, 1998; Hewison, 2006). Fitful democratic reforms
stretching back to the 1970s meant these private interests were able
to outflank the formerly dominant state bureaucracy and press their
interests more directly through a pervasive system of money politics,
to become the financiers of parties rather than the clients of bureaucrats (Anderson, 1990; Hewison, 1993).

A similar transformation came in Indonesia when the state capitalism of Sukarno was replaced with the more globally oriented market
authoritarianism of Soeharto in the mid-1960s. While the rise to
prominence of technocrats in key economic ministries in the Soeharto
government was widely seen by neoliberal economists as a triumph of
rationality over politics, these coexisted with a pervasive apparatus of
security and repression and a vast network of state-owned enterprises
that stood astride the commanding heights of the economy (Robison,
1986, 1988). Ideas of technocratic and managerial rule were used by
the regime to legitimise the bypassing of representative and competitive politics in the name of protecting policy efficiency and economic
growth against the demands of vested interest (see Moertopo, 1973).

The speed of market reforms increased in the 1980s, including
financial sector deregulation, some easing of trade monopolies and the
privatisation of some key state activities. These benefited a growing
group of business conglomerates who increasingly saw the economic
authority of the state as a constraint and its lucrative monopolies as

prizes. But the reforms did not open the door to a liberal transformation of the economy or the relationship between business and the state. Instead, the reforms enabled powerful business interests to seize former state monopolies without a comprehensive liberalisation of the economy and to access the benefits of a deregulated financial and banking sector. Trading and manufacturing cartels reliant on forestry concessions, import monopolies and government contracts were preserved in private hands while the newly liberalised finance sector opened the door to investors who were unconstrained by rules about intra-group lending and capital adequacy ratios. Among the new private banks, no distinction existed between lenders and borrowers. Most importantly, privatisation meant that public monopolies were transformed into private monopolies while key state enterprises became the conduits through which state funds haemorrhaged into private hands by subsidising the costs of their activities and providing discretionary credit (Robison and Hadiz, 2004: 69–144).

In Cambodia, market reforms occurred later, following decades of war, upheaval and failed attempts at collectivisation. Until the mid-1990s, 90 per cent of Cambodians made their living from farming, fishing or hunting and gathering. Bloody experiments in forced collectivisation of agriculture and forestry in the late 1970s had caused a huge death toll and widespread famine, and were followed in the 1980s by a gradual return to household-based production on family plots. Other resources – including forests, fisheries and water resources – were regarded as commons and used according to customary practices. Many forest resources were in practice inaccessible due to continued insurgency and a massive landmine problem.

As the insurgency wound down at the end of the Cold War, these common resources were regarded by the incumbent Cambodian government as opportunities for dispensing patronage to all important military and local government leaders, in the run-up to elections organised by the United Nations. As forests, water resources and fisheries became more accessible following international mine-clearing operations, they were awarded to firms as concessions for resource extraction. The award of these concessions generally involved the payment of huge bribes to political leaders, and the eviction of customary users from concession areas was abrupt and violent. While key international donors, notably the World Bank and the IMF, deplored the violence and illegality associated with these events, they were favourably disposed towards the privatisation policies themselves, regarding the imposition of what Andrew Cock calls an 'industrial model' of development on Cambodian forests, for example, as an appropriate resource management strategy (Cock, 2007).

The resources generated, in terms of profits, bribes, royalties and kickbacks, were used over the next decade to build the basis of oligarchic rule in post-conflict Cambodia. Not only did they make political leaders and well-connected Cambodian tycoons enormously wealthy but they also provided slush funds to pay for extravagant election campaigns. The Cambodian People's Party sponsored rural development projects across the country and voters were lined up, village by village, and given personal gifts in return for their loyalty at forthcoming polls (Hughes, 2003, 2006).

Thus, after more than three decades of market reforms, development agencies and donor governments found themselves confronted with widespread consolidation of illiberal politics and new forms of oligarchy based on the expropriation of markets. The question was whether these constituted a transitional phenomenon or new and sustainable forms of market states. Would they be undermined by the evolving structural demands of markets or by the emergence of new social or political forces? Would they be neutralised by the efforts of technocrats to impose new market institutions and forms of neoliberal governance?

From markets to the market state

By the late 1990s, many of the regimes that had arisen on the basis of market reforms and globalisation in the 1980s and 1990s appeared to be experiencing difficulties. In sub-Saharan Africa, it was hard to see how predatory rulers could survive in the face of deepening poverty and economic decline. In Russia, the heady days of excess in the early 1990s gave way to economic crisis and the near collapse of the banking and financial system. And the devastating impact of the Asian Economic Crisis in 1997–98 signalled, for many Western observers, including within the IMF and the World Bank, the ultimate triumph of markets and the end of those Asian political regimes that had refused to embrace their discipline (Friedman, 1997).

Economic crises and ongoing poverty were seen by development banks and organisations as an opportunity to impose on hitherto recalcitrant governments programmes of institutional reform, state building and 'good governance' defined by the practices and values of the market and which included reforms in public sector management and in judicial reform to enable predictable and consistent rule of law (World Bank, 1991, 2002a). It was assumed that the behaviour of politicians and business could be altered by incentives and sanctions built into institutional reforms by their technocrat designers, not least those in the World Bank and the IMF. At the same time, there was a belief that crisis and failure would be a strong lesson to governments and others in developing countries of the costs of 'bad governance' and the benefits of market reforms and predictable and accountable public administration. It was regarded as an environment where 'champions' of neoliberal reform might be found within the government and among civil society to support such institutional reform.

As we shall see, such institutional reforms took root only in certain circumstances. The key factor is whether powerful social interests could be mobilised behind the governance agenda. It had been widely assumed that business itself would eventually tire of the unpredictability of the predatory political circumstances within which they had been nurtured and would seek the certainty of rules and rational governance (see Harris, 1988). However, emerging bourgeoisies were to be part of a variety of political and social outcomes, including consolidation of systems of disorganised and predatory capitalism and where liberal ideas and democracies played little part. The question that emerges from this observation is how we explain why new political oligarchies, generally embedded in both the institutions of the state and in the world of business, shape the rules of markets and specific forms of state authority.

Nowhere were attempts to deal with problems of poverty and 'bad governance' by institutional reform and 'good governance' more intensively applied than in sub-Saharan Africa. Here, Western donors and development agencies confronted what Harrison (2006: 109) described as 'a new political class that reproduces itself through "neoliberal clientism"'. This was a political class that had used programmes of market liberalisation as well as large inflows of development assistance beginning from the 1980s to consolidate political ascendancy and economic authority within client networks. Yet, the enthusiasm among Western governments and donors for new 'champions' promising public sector reform and an end to corruption, including

Museveni in Uganda, Rawlings in Ghana, Chiluba in Zambia and Kibaki in Kenya, indicated a belief that all this could be ended. Indeed, as Harrison observed, the new governments and elites widely adopted the institutional practices and discourses of the market and of new public management: pervasive auditing, reporting, outsourcing and contracting-out and so on. However, as he also notes:

> local officials perceive and evaluate the introduction of neoliberal practice from grounded places. That is, the existing practices of authority frame how one might relate to the introduction of neoliberal reforms. It is from these existing social practices that neo-liberalism becomes a resource – a set of possibilities – to borrow, challenge or ignore.
>
> (Harrison, 2010: 130)

The same principles operated at the national levels where the corrupt disposal of state enterprises, leakage of finance from large banks and corruption in procurement as well as plunder in the Congo and elsewhere have all been essential elements in the way the new 'champions' of neoliberal reform have reinforced the politics of ethnic allegiances, patronage and corruption (van de Walle, 2001; Tangri and Mwenda, 2001, 2003; Harrison, 2005, 2006, 2010: 140–2).[3]

The African experience suggests several seemingly paradoxical influences in the politics of neoliberal reform. Harrison argues that while the neoliberal experiment has implicitly assumed the presence of a strong state, it has been forced to work in Africa within a highly clientelist political structure. It cannot be said to have carved out spaces for itself within these highly chaotic political environments to deny entry to cronyism, patronage and corruption. This raises the question of whether regulated market economies and effective market institutions can be built on the basis of political systems that are predatory and chaotic. Are more authoritarian and 'rational' forms of state authority a prerequisite for market economies and market societies?

While Harrison acknowledges this proposition he also argues that, while it cannot be said that neoliberalism has simply been 'hijacked' by client politics, the relationship between the two is not so strange. Certain types of 'predictable' corruption and clientelism might not be entirely incompatible with neoliberalism and might not be bad for business or investment (Harrison, 2006: 110–13). This invites some recognition that the real origins of markets can generally be found where chaos and corruption, rather than any pristine notion of 'good governance' and technocratic autonomy, as proposed by neoliberals, were the incubating factors.

A similar approach is taken by Paul Hutchcroft (1998) in his analysis of the Philippines, where decades of market capitalism and efforts at building effective regulatory institutions have failed to make inroads into what he calls a system of 'booty capitalism'. The persistence of this form of capitalism, Hutchcroft argues, has resulted from the special political relationship between powerful and cohesive business families and an incoherent state. Economic growth, in this situation, he proposes, reinforced the power of social interests resistant to reforms designed to break up rent-seeking coalitions and impose general rules on business. In contrast, it is claimed, the rise of a modern rational state is more likely where power resides, at least in the early stages, with a class of office-holders who are the main beneficiaries of rents extracted from a politically disorganised business class. Here the state is assumed to possess the autonomy to impose reform and nurture a private sector more likely to tire of the uncertainties of rents and seek more formal modes of economic governance (see Hutchcroft, 1998: 45–64).

A different path to oligarchy is offered by the case of Russia. As indicated earlier, the large and powerful Russian state had indeed been the driving force for market reforms, largely through its programme of divestment of state assets to private investors. Fears that this would simply result in an ongoing era of robber barons were dismissed by Anatoly Chubais, one of the technocratic architects of the 1990s shares-for-loans privatisation that ushered in this period. He claimed that despite the chaos, corruption and inequity that had accompanied it, not only was 'shock therapy' the only possible way of creating private property but also the oligarchs that emerged would themselves increasingly tire of the arbitrary and discretionary authority that made their ascendancy possible and see that moving on to the next stage requires a system based on rules that ensure their general interests (cited in Ostrovsky, 2003, 2004). Marxist analysts also argued that the arbitrary handover of state assets in Russia to well-placed individuals in a process of unconstrained 'primitive accumulation' was essential to the early stages of capitalist development in the country. They proposed that this world of political deals, gangsters and violence had its own structural limits and would be cured only if the state secured the position of the oligarchs through property rights and via the increasing interest of business in an orderly system of regulated market capitalism (Holdstrom and Smith, 2000).

Both these arguments assume some sort of structural imperative presumably backed by technocrats or a new business class tired of uncertainty and the increasing constraints of political control. However, in the Russian case, neither the newly emerged oligarchies nor the state itself was to become the agent of a fully fledged neoliberal revolution. The key factor here was the existence of a powerful and pervasive state nomenklatura that sought to protect its institutional base in the state apparatus and to exert its authority over the oligarchs. President Putin moved against the oligarchs, confiscating several large conglomerates and imprisoning key business leaders. This was an action designed neither to roll back the market nor to impose the rules of the market upon unruly and predatory forces. It was designed to contain them within the ambit of the state itself, to renationalise many of the commanding heights of capitalism and to prevent the possibility that the rise of an unconstrained oligarchy might spill over into a broader political challenges to the state and its political and bureaucratic apparatchiks within the new parliamentary institutions.

In Latin America, neoliberal reforms were to be the basis of challenges to entrenched regimes in several countries, although not in the way expected by donors in the development aid industry. New reformist leaders did not represent a progressive bourgeoisie but emerged from the peripheries of established elites themselves. Among these were Alberto Fujimori and Carlos Bolona in Peru, Carlos Menem in Argentina, Miguel Rodriguez in Venezuela and Fernando Collor in Brazil. They saw fiscal austerity, privatisation and deregulation in trade and investment as an opportunity to undermine the base of entrenched elites, in patronage and cartels, and to construct new political bases in league with provincial and middle and lower ranking classes together with emerging corporate and financial interests.

What emerged was an amalgam of neoliberalism and populism that dispensed with earlier forms of corporatist alliances or settlements, including with labour unions. The new rulers constructed plebiscitary relationships instead with the unorganised poor and formerly marginal elements of the lower middle classes. This anti-organisational bent, argues Weyland (2003: 1098), had important affinities with neoliberalism: 'As populism wants to protect the unity of the people against politicking factions and selfish elites, so neoliberalism seeks to protect the equilibrium of the market against the machinations of mercantilist rent-seekers'. However close these organisational affinities, neoliberal populism was in reality to be most effective as a vehicle for enabling new elites to replace vested interests previously ascendant in the political system but without a reconstitution of state authority on the basis of practices and values of the market.

In much of Southeast Asia, the Asian Financial Crisis of 1997–1998 offered the World Bank, the IMF and other development organisations an unprecedented opportunity to impose institutional reforms envisaged in the World Bank's *World Development Report 1997*. It was assumed that economic crises had brought lessons about the costs of ignoring the discipline of the markets (see Camdessus, 1997, 1998). Almost immediately after the crisis the IMF and other development organisations began to impose programmes for reforms in governance in return for huge financial bailouts, especially in Thailand, South Korea and Indonesia but also in the Philippines. These included special corruption watchdogs, arms-length procurement practices, transparency regulations, increased property rights, capacity training for officials and remuneration strategies as well as programmes of democratic reform and political and administrative decentralisation.[4] It was envisaged that the political balance in the policy struggles would swing to the technocrats who could now move ahead with institutional reforms that would neutralise distributional coalitions.[5]

It was certainly true in post-crisis Thailand that the new post-crisis government of Chavalit Yongchaiyudh embraced neoliberal reforms with enthusiasm (Hewison, 2005: 314–17). Ironically, the main challenge to this neoliberal reforming state came from within business itself which achieved its most complete ascendancy over the state following the electoral victory of the Thai Rak Thai (TRT) party of new Prime Minister, Thaksin Shinawatra. However, rather than demanding more market and institutional reforms, those elements of business dominant in the TRT were reacting against the hard-line neoliberal reforms of immediate post-crisis governments as beleaguered domestic business interests sought to consolidate their position *vis-à-vis* the advance of global markets. Policies were put in place to stem the flow of external corporate takeovers and to slow the pace of privatisations and corporate reform. At the same time, the political ascendancy of business was consolidated in an increasingly centralised system of money politics appealing to the poor where a new social contract to draft broad political support included highly populist measures for health insurance and village-level grants. In an important sense, the Thai bourgeoisie adopted a Fujimori solution to their problems (Pasuk and Baker, 2004; Hewison, 2005). Ironically, neoliberals and their technocrat associates found themselves in alliance with metropolitan middle classes and conservative elites gathered around the monarchy and the army in reaction against this business-led populist revolution.

In Indonesia, the Asian Financial Crisis of 1997–1998 not only resulted in economic disarray but was also a key factor in the collapse of the Soeharto regime itself. This led to a dramatic shift to democratic politics and the liberation of the media that had long been controlled by the state. It also provided an opportunity for the World Bank and the IMF to drive a raft of substantial reforms through the administrative and political institutions of Indonesia. An ambitious programme of bank recapitalisation was expected to clear out undercapitalised and speculative financial interests. Extensive reforms in public sector management and changes to the judiciary, including the establishment of an anti-corruption commission, were complemented by a far-reaching programme of decentralisation that shifted administrative and political authority into the hands of provincial and sub-provincial parliaments (Hadiz, 2010).

Nevertheless, old power relationships demonstrated great resilience in the face of these shocks. Although ultimately forced out of sectors like finance and banking, Indonesian conglomerates moved into booming resources and property sectors, retaining the essentially predatory relationships with politicians and state officials even though these were now located within parliaments and a more diffuse and disorganised state apparatus. Technically bankrupted business groups held onto their key assets by emptying their banks and sending the cash overseas, stalling foreign creditors or warehousing their debt with the government agencies responsible for the recapitalisation of banks, and fighting efforts to seize assets or prosecute them by using corrupt courts, effectively socialising the costs of their losses (Lindsay, 2000; Hamilton-Hart, 2002; Robison and Hadiz, 2004: 187–222; Butt, 2012).

Despite the collapse of centralised authoritarian rule and the introduction of political and administrative reforms, the same systems of business–state relations were reproduced within the new systems of democratic and decentralised politics, albeit within an expanded cast of characters, across a wider range of alliances and within a more disorganised system of money politics, extending down into the provinces and sub-provinces (Hadiz, 2004, 2007; Djani, 2013). Although reformers now had opportunities to publicise and prosecute their agendas in a way not possible under the former regime, their primary targets – including the judiciary, the bureaucracy and the parliament – remained stubbornly resilient within the new institutional frameworks (Lindsey, 2000; Butt, 2012).

Where the new bourgeoisie became frustrated with the post-authoritarian state it was not universally because it provided little certainty or predictability but because the democratic institutions meant that popular forces could obstruct the plans of business. The solution to the existing situation was not always seen by local interests in terms of a more effectively regulated liberal market economy. The model of state-sponsored oligarchy presented by China and Russia, a sort of fascism, is also attractive. Comparing China to Indonesia, for example, former Vice President (and prominent businessman), Jusuf Kalla, recently observed:

> China's strength is that it can plan and implement. Our system, which is too democratic with too much individual freedom that often disregards the rights of others, has made it difficult for us to build infrastructure ... As long as individual right is above public responsibility, we will not progress ... That's the only problem we have now.
>
> (Suparno, 2007)

Does the West really want to confront the elephants in the room?

Development agencies and banks that seek to impose institutional or policy reform may collide with other ideological, geo-strategic or commercial interests within the West that have different agendas. Programmes aimed at reforming the public sector, ending corruption, tackling poverty or mitigating human rights abuses, for example, may not suit the priorities of governments or commercial interests in the West.

It is clear that the rise of illiberal regimes and oligarchic power in developing countries has offered commercial advantages to investors and exporters in the West. Globalisation, ironically, has meant an opportunity for investors to seek competitive advantages within different systems of governance, where the political weakness of social welfare and environmental lobbies and civil rights mean looser regulation, lower taxes and labour costs. The loose and often disorganised regulatory environment of developing countries often provides opportunities for the corporate sector in the West to escape regulatory constraints on financial markets, health and environmental standards, labour laws and business practice that persist in Western countries where residual social-democratic institutions still survive (see, for example, Simpson, 2008).

Despite potential costs of political uncertainty and chaotic infrastructure, Western investors have been able to coexist with corrupt and unstable regimes. Risks can be offset where the potential bonanza offered by the capture of rents is high, as illustrated in the financial feeding frenzy that directed huge flows of funds into increasingly speculative Asian markets in the years preceding the Asian economic crisis (Wade, 1998; Kristof and Sanger, 1999). Such risks can be lessened by hedging through complex derivative instruments and by the direct support of government-owned import/export banks and insurance providers and where the IMF might be expected to come to the rescue, bailing out imprudent investors rather than allowing them to face the consequences of bad decisions. It is ironic that one editorial in the right-wing *Asian Wall Street Journal* (1997: 10) characterised the IMF as nothing less than a form of socialist international following its decision to provide substantial bailout funds to South Korea, Indonesia and Thailand after the economic crisis of 1997–1998.

Development agencies can also collide with the priorities of Ministries of Foreign Affairs and Defence in their own governments for whom global geo-strategic and political interests are paramount. Regimes that are constructed on 'bad governance' and, hence, are the target of reformers can also be the very regimes that provide the political muscle to eliminate domestic or regional political movements that are radical or social-democrat in nature even where they preside over poor development records and social repression. And they can be allies in struggles for global influence, large arms purchasers or the suppliers of strategic energy and mineral resources. During the Cold

War, a range of anti-communist dictatorships in Latin America and the Middle East remained close allies of the West despite their poor development and human rights credentials.

Governments and business in the West remain highly defensive where reformers target 'bad governance' among important political or economic allies. It is instructive, for example, that the 'Asian Values' justification for highly autocratic political and economic behaviour by governments in the Asian region struck such a sympathetic cord in conservative and government circles in the West in the 1990s (see Robison, 1996; Rodan, 1996). We have already noted the attractions of the Singapore model to neoliberals.

In a different vein, and more recently, the readiness of the European Union to support Central Asian rulers, who are not well known for their democratic practices, is equally striking. The acceptance of governance 'reforms', which were characterised by many critics as mere window dressing, as steps on the way to respecting human rights, appeared in no small way influenced by the interests of EU countries in accessing the oil and gas reserves that are present in the Central Asian republics (see Hoffmann, 2010).

The reaction within the neoliberal camp to the rise of more democratic governments and the increasing disorganisation of authority that often accompanied such changes is also important given the pervasive influence of neoliberalism in development organisations and economic ministries of Western governments. Democratic transitions are unpredictable and there is a clear apprehension about the possible implications for the interests of private investors. In the case of Indonesia several influential neoliberal economists have been critical of the growing influence of 'distributional coalitions' and the growing confusion of authority in the new democratic and decentralised political system. This has been compared in a highly nostalgic way to the certainty and enforcement of property rights under the former Soeharto regime, and even to the greater predictability of corruption in those days (Duncan and McLeod, 2007).

The relationship is also a two-way street. As Mick Moore (2001: 385) has argued, the 'political underdevelopment of much of the South also results from the ways in which Southern states have been created and political authority shaped through economic and political interactions with the wealthier countries of the North'. He points to the way various regimes and rulers in developing countries have benefited, not only from aid and loans from the developed world but also from their ability to launder their wealth and to invest and hide it through the banks and other financial institutions of the West.

At the same time, income from oil and mining in particular has provided many regimes with a degree of autonomy, not only from the demands of their own citizens but from the demands for 'good governance' inherent in the requirements of global governance (Moore, 2001; Bates, 2006). Close relationships with foreign firms (particularly in some of the weaker African states) have been a basis for the funding of predatory regimes and also have enabled such regimes to conduct offensives against old patronage networks and insurgencies and to deal with other states and multilateral agencies (Reno, 1997).

In more recent times, the struggle for reform in the development arena has become influenced by new struggles for global economic and political hegemony, particularly as China entered the arena. It is significant that Chinese investment, especially in Africa, carries no demands for broader reforms (Watts, 2006).[6] As Western donor nations are forced into increasing competition with China for the support of national governments and as the attractions of the Chinese model itself draw the attention of powerful interests in developing countries, the pressures on development policymakers to allow 'hard-nosed' strategic and commercial interest to take precedence over reformist agendas are certain to be increased.

It is clear that the frustrations that have accompanied programmes of institution building and 'good governance' as well as the disappointment of efforts to cultivate progressive forces have become too much for many in the development industry. There has been a retreat from prescriptive approaches and a lowering of expectations. Merilee Grindle has identified the overwhelming odds facing those who seek to build good governance universally and suggests that development organisations should lower their ambitions for governance reform – an approach that has become known as 'good enough governance' (Grindle, 2004b: 7).

Others have emphasised the need to target fewer countries with governance reform policies, and focus on those countries that have already made progress with implementing reform. The emphasis on countries making progress has led to the use of selectivity criteria for allocating aid, on the basis of which partner countries are selected. For instance, the US Millennium Challenge Account simply proposed to exclude from its development programmes any country that did not already meet its governance criteria (see Hout, 2007; Chhotray and Hulme, 2009).

In reassessing the impact of forms of so-called neopatrimonialism, Brinkerhoff and Goldsmith (2004: 5) propose that worthwhile market reforms can be achieved within existing clientelist institutions and forms of governance. In its 2010 study of governance, the Centre for the Future State, a research centre based in UK, argued that rather than trying to impose specific ideas of 'good governance' on the regimes of developing countries, Western governments and their agencies should discover ways they can work within existing forms of governance and institutions rather than seeking to impose their own (Centre for the Future State, 2010).

Despite their retreat from the more strident institutional orthodoxy of the World Bank, these analysts still see institutions as the primary engine of change through their influence on individual behaviour. This contrasts with our focus on the question of where institutions come from and how they are shaped and our view that they are forged in conflicts between social interests to define the rules of markets that are ultimately about power and how it is distributed and organised. However, tackling the problems of development at their political roots is even more difficult for reformers than trying to build institutions and systems of governance. They confront the central paradox that the spread of markets can create and consolidate forces whose interest are embedded in predatory and illiberal institutions and render even more impotent those forces bringing a progressive agenda.

3
Development Agencies and the Political Economy Turn

Introduction

As we showed in earlier chapters, donor agencies started to realise in the 1990s that development policy involves more than adherence to macroeconomic fundamentals, which had been the major precept of the Washington Consensus. The awareness that non-economic factors were important produced a wave of publications on the centrality of 'governance' and led to a focus on institutions.

Following the World Bank's approach to governance, many development agencies have tended to orientate their governance programmes on relatively technical issues, such as public sector management, public finance and decentralisation. In their support of governance reform programmes, the agencies were preoccupied with the sequencing of reforms rather than with the concrete impacts that such reforms were having on the power relations in the countries concerned (cf. Robison, 2009).

In this chapter we discuss the struggle of the donor community with the application of political economy analysis to governance issues. In particular, the ensuing discussion focuses on the paradox that donor agencies stress the need to engage in political economy analyses but, at the same time, appear to be largely unable to use the insights derived from such analyses. Our discussion focuses on three cases: the UK's Department for International Development (DFID), the Dutch Directorate-General for International Cooperation (DGIS) and the World Bank.

We show that an understanding of why development agencies are apparently unable to apply the outcomes of political economy analysis

36

requires a theoretical interpretation of the very political economy of the aid agencies themselves. This theoretical interpretation needs to take into account the way in which donor agencies function in relation to their environment, as well as the main operational features of those agencies. On the basis of the notions of epistemic communities and organisational incentives, derived from the disciplines of international relations and public administration, we argue that the difficulty of development agencies to use political economy approaches stems from their conception of what is proper development policy. For most agencies, development is about improving (poor) peoples' livelihoods, in terms of either income or social development indicators (with the Millennium Development Goals as the pinnacle of the current policy consensus). Development policies are conceived, first and foremost, in terms of the instruments to achieve these targets. Agencies are primarily interested in 'doing development', which implies implementing projects and programmes successfully. Although they are concerned *about* the political context in which they operate, they feel they should not themselves be concerned *with* politics in their partner countries. The development agencies continue to operate effectively as 'anti-politics machines' (cf. Ferguson, 1990) and this is why they experience an almost insurmountable difficulty in taking political assessments seriously.

The next section develops a general framework, the aim of which is to make sense of the political economy of donor agencies. The three subsequent sections then analyse the instruments for political economy analysis that were introduced by the three development agencies mentioned above: the Drivers of Change adopted by DFID, the Strategic Governance and Corruption Analysis (SGACA) developed by DGIS and the new thinking on political economy analysis, policy reform and political risk advanced by the World Bank. The final section contains some conclusions.

Understanding donor agencies

The continuing discussion on the purposes of aid indicates that the jury is still out on the question as to what motivates governments to give aid. As Carol Lancaster (2007: 12–18) has made clear in her much-cited work on foreign aid, 'development' is clearly only one among various purposes of aid. Despite this ambiguity at the level of government decision-makers, it is probably safe to say that development agencies are on the whole highly goal-oriented: to a large extent, the 'institutional ethos' (Unsworth, 2009: 890) of the agencies derives from the commitment of their staff to 'making poverty history' and improving the quality of life of people in the poor parts of the world. On the basis of a set of key policy documents of leading international development agencies, former Overseas Development Institute Director Simon Maxwell has usefully summarised the key elements of the current development agenda as a 'new meta-narrative'. According to Maxwell, the new mantra of development assistance is characterised by acceptance of the Millennium Development Goals as an 'over-arching framework', linking these to national Poverty Reduction Strategies, which are to be endorsed by the World Bank and IMF, 'sound' macroeconomic policies and trade liberalisation, proper public expenditure management and harmonised aid aimed at improving governance (Maxwell, 2005: 1).

Development agencies can be understood as the quintessential specimens of an 'epistemic community'. According to Peter Haas (1992: 3), an epistemic community is 'a network of professionals with recognized expertise and competence in a particular domain and an authoritative claim to policy-relevant knowledge within that domain or issue-area'. Epistemic communities have several characteristics that set them apart from looser networks. Haas (1992: 3) has mentioned four key features: they share (1) norms and principles; (2) 'causal beliefs' linking policies to desired results; (3) criteria to determine what constitutes valid knowledge; and (4) a 'policy enterprise – that is, a set of common practices associated with a set of problems to which their professional competence is directed, presumably out of the conviction that human welfare will be enhanced as a consequence'.

The activities of development agencies clearly fit the picture of the epistemic community drawn by Haas. Development agencies are made up of professionals who engage in the common endeavour to reduce or eradicate poverty and empower the poorest parts of the population in developing countries. They work on the basis of a shared set of understandings of and values about processes of development. Their objectives, involving social, economic and political reform, are seen to require long-term investments of finance and human resources, the results of which cannot always be readily established. The nature of the work of development agencies implies that such agencies are subject to particular incentive structures. Scholars have emphasised, for quite some time already, that the incentive structure of development agencies has many characteristics of a 'principal-agent problem' (Killick, 1998; Gibson et al., 2005: 43–4). The main issue is that development agencies, which are the responsible 'agents' for the implementation of development policies, may have preferences that are not identical to those of their 'principals' (government, parliament or the electorate at large). Development agencies may be motivated more by considerations of budget maximisation than by providing results at the lowest possible cost. Moreover, their professional ethos may lead them to get involved in programmes that are, in the terms used by Andrew Natsios (see Chapter 1), more transformational, but also contain a higher risk of failure. Since the selection of failing programmes usually does not have budgetary consequences, this selection is, moreover, subject to 'moral hazard' problems (Gibson et al., 2005: 42–3).

One important implication of dealing with complex realities is that it is hard for development agencies to define and measure their output. Although the attention for aid effectiveness – epitomised in the 'Paris Declaration on Aid Effectiveness' (2005) and the 'Accra Agenda for Action' (2008) – has recently come high on the international agenda, the main instruments for aid agencies to establish staff performance remain the commitment and disbursement of funds – 'moving money', as Easterly (2002: 228) called it –, the management of projects and programmes, and the production of reports and memos (Carlsson et al., 1994: 5; cf. Gibson et al., 2005: 134–5, 154–6).[1] To the extent that assessment of results is possible, project and programme evaluations are usually very time-consuming and their findings get published long after the fact (Gibson et al., 2005: 151–4).

The absence of clear success indicators implies that the incentives for staff of aid bureaucracies tend to be linked to the observable outputs that were mentioned above: disbursement activity, management and written work. This brings about an orientation of staff on technical aspects of the work, as their advancement within the organisation depends on assessments of their performance in financial and project or programme management. Moreover, as evidenced in a study of Dutch development assistance, the success of staff depends on the visibility of the policy papers they produce: an in-depth ethnographic study of Dutch development cooperation cited the expression 'those who write remain' to indicate the importance of written output for staff advancement (Van Gastel and Nuijten, 2005: 98). On the basis of interviews with staff at the Swedish International Development Cooperation Agency (SIDA) Gibson et al. (2005: 144) concluded that there are few incentives for staff to learn from past activities and gain in-depth knowledge about the country they are working in.

Not only internal characteristics of development agencies lead to the adoption of a technocratic outlook among their staff. Changes in the external environment of donor agencies have contributed to the intensification of the technocratic approach. All of the major public development organisations are funded through the budgets of national governments or are themselves international public organisations. As such, they are hostage to specific kinds of bureaucratic processes that may be explained in the context of the new public management framework. Development agencies, no less than any other public organisation, have increasingly been forced to operate on the basis of market principles and values. Moreover, as part of general requirements of 'accountability', governments need to demonstrate how the tax dollars and euros spent on development assistance are effective – something that is not helped by periodic revelations of waste or misuse of funds spent on the citizens of other countries. Thus, apart from episodic expenditures on humanitarian tragedies, politicians are required to explain to suspicious publics that development budgets are effective ways of achieving national interests. As Eyben noted, these pressures also represent the focus on risk in Western bureaucracies and the rise of the audit culture (Eyben, 2005: 100–1).

The result has been the construction of a regime of review and assessment in which measures of success are defined by processes rather than development outcomes and expressed in quantitative and easily demonstrated terms. It is a process that favours measurable indicators such as the supply of physical projects, 'good governance' and institutions. Thus, considerable energy has been injected, for example, into measuring 'good governance' (cf. Kaufmann et al., 2007). Further, the Millennium Development Goals provide a set of 'key performance indicators' for officials that require ways of measuring levels of poverty or illiteracy. The construction of schools, delivery of training courses, provision of information, travel and workshops are all useful measures for quantitative review. Thus, institution-building projects are ideal for such review in the new public management model. The energies of the development agencies are shifted from tackling the causal problems of development to that of devising methodologies for measuring performance and selecting the sorts of activities that are best measured.

So-called 'new development management' (Cooke and Dar, 2008; cf. Copestake and Williams, 2012) is an application of new management techniques that aim to minimise risk and control the behaviour of public servants. On the one hand, new development management has resulted in the generalisation of evaluations to the extent that they have almost assumed the characteristics of a disease labelled 'evaluitis' (Frey, 2007). On the other hand, it has led to the introduction of new instruments for enhancing accountability. Examples of such new instruments are the Public Service Agreements for international development in the UK and the spread of a 'counter-bureaucracy' aimed at the management of aid programmes in the US. Natsios has pointed at the pernicious effects of the bureaucratisation:

> This regulatory apparatus has created an incentive structure that has led to an emphasis on process over program substance and, in so doing, has produced a perverse bureaucratic result; as the career staff has declined in size absolutely and proportionately to the size of the aid budget, the compliance side of aid has taken over management and decision making at [USAID].
>
> (Natsios, 2010: 5)

Under the influence of pressures from the external environment, regulatory and new management techniques have been internalised by development agencies and have become accepted as normal elements of 'good housekeeping'. Over time, new development management has become institutionalised and the range of instruments it produced has resulted in a further deepening of the inherent technocratic orientation of the agencies.

All in all, it can be concluded that development agencies, as rather technocratic 'agents' responsible for the organisation of development assistance, are not well placed to engage with more fundamental analyses of the political economy of partner countries that may be felt desirable by their 'principals'. On the one hand, development agencies are likely to resist the implications of political economy analyses because of their institutional ethos, which makes them concerned about the least developed parts of the world where the institutional frameworks are weakest. Political economy analyses could force them to become more risk-averse and avoid working in situations where 'transformational' opportunities may be greatest. On the other hand, the promotion of political economy analyses by the leadership at headquarters does not seem to correspond with the organisational incentives provided to individual staff members, as these are linked to disbursement, management and reporting rather than fundamental investigation of the realities in aid-recipient countries.

Drivers of Change[2]

In 1997, Claire Short, Secretary of State for International Development in the Blair government, presented the first major policy statement on UK development cooperation in over 20 years. This policy document stressed the importance of improving governance: it announced measures 'to build sound and accountable government which is the foundation of economic growth and poverty elimination allowing poor and disadvantaged people to achieve their civil, political, economic, social and cultural rights' (Secretary of State for International Development, 1997: 32). The UK's targets for governance, which were perceived to be instrumental for achieving the main goals of international development policies, were cast in terms of seven 'key capabilities for the state' (DFID, 2001: 12):

- the establishment of a political system that enables all people to influence government policy;
- macroeconomic stability and facilitation of private sector investment and trade;
- pro-poor policies;
- effective public service delivery;
- personal safety and security, and access to justice;
- the creation of accountable national security arrangements and mechanisms for conflict resolution;
- the combating of corruption.

This listing makes clear that 'governance' in the early days of the Blair government was defined in largely instrumental terms and had a strong focus on policies of aid-recipient countries.

The need for a political economy approach to governance issues was identified at the headquarters of the UK's DFID in 1999, when Roger

Wilson, Head of the Governance Department, conceived a research project on 'responsiveness of political systems to poverty reduction' (Moore and Putzel, 1999). According to Wilson (2002: part 3), poor performance of countries on poverty reduction required an explanation related to the functioning of political systems, with particular attention to the role of accountability. The concern with politics brought DFID's Governance Department to develop an approach called Change Forecasting, which actually contained the first steps towards the Drivers of Change methodology. The objective of this approach – which, according to Wilson, would operate best at the sector level, but could also be applied at the country level – was to identify who among the political elite in developing countries would be interested in governance reforms, and who would not be committed to change (Wilson, 2002: part 6).

On the basis of these first steps, DFID launched the so-called Drivers of Change framework with an analysis of the 'drivers of pro-poor change' in Bangladesh in 2002 (Duncan et al., 2002). The direct reason for the introduction of Drivers of Change was the feeling at DFID that it would not be sufficient for donor agencies 'to bring about change through technically sound programmes, supported in country by individual champions of reform or change' (DFID, 2004: 1). In addition to such programmes, it was argued, knowledge would be required about governance realities on the ground in developing countries, in particular related to the role of formal and informal institutions and 'underlying structural features' shaping governance practices.

The philosophy behind the Drivers of Change methodology was to examine:

> 'what is driving change' in the countries where DFID is active. This is to address the fact that, 'DFID and other donors find it easier to say "what" needs to be done to reduce poverty than "how" to help make it happen'. By better understanding how change occurs within specific contexts, it is hypothesised that DFID's programming decisions will be better equipped to respond to this 'how' question and help bring about pro-poor change. DoC therefore emphasises DFID's need to understand economic, political and social contexts, in other words, the application of political economy analysis to formulation of donor strategy and implementation.
>
> (Warrener, 2004: 1)

Between June 2003 and September 2004, a Drivers of Change team functioned within the Policy Division at DFID headquarters, which primarily served to facilitate analyses at country level and did not impose a single methodology. After September 2004, a much smaller policy team was set up only for coordination activities (Dahl-Østergaard et al., 2005: 4). Thus, the Drivers of Change programme typically led to the commissioning of analyses by DFID country offices from teams of independent local and international consultants. Altogether, consultants have produced some 25 reports[3] that all followed the programme's broad conceptual model.

By analysing three different aspects of economic, political and social contexts (agents, structural features and institutions), the Drivers of Change methodology attempted to uncover the factors that contribute to or impede change. Agents are individuals and organisations pursuing particular interests, including political elites, the judiciary, the military, civil society organisations and the media. Structural features relate to 'deeply embedded' factors as the history of state formation, natural resources, economic and social structures, and urbanisation. Institutions are the formal and informal 'rules governing the behaviour of agents', and range from laws and official procedures to social and cultural norms (DFID, 2004: 1). As Mustaq Khan (2005: 38) has noted in a review of various Drivers of Change studies, the common assumption underlying those studies seems to have been that certain 'good governance reforms' are a prerequisite for further development and transformation in aid-receiving countries. The main issues appeared to be the sequencing of reforms and the identification of the change agents to bring about such governance reforms.

Assessments of the Drivers of Change approach have pointed at various weaknesses that limited the usefulness of the framework. In a review of the first 20 reports, Adrian Leftwich (2006: 17–20) focused on the lack of rigour underlying the Drivers of Change studies (cf. Khan, 2005: 5–6). He noted that the studies performed under the broad umbrella of Drivers of Change displayed considerable variance in the use of central concepts such as agents, structural features and institutions. Moreover, Leftwich argued, the studies did not produce a convincing view on possible dynamics of change, as the interrelations among agents, institutions and structures were not well specified. Finally, Leftwich indicated that there was not a clear, shared understanding among the Drivers of Change analyses of what 'political economy' actually is.

Various commentators have argued that several factors limited the applicability of the Drivers of Change approach to programming exercises and concrete policy decisions (Dahl-Østergaard et al., 2005; Thornton and Cox, 2005). Importantly, the timing of Drivers of Change studies was often not well aligned with the preparation of DFID's country programmes. Further, many Drivers of Change analyses proved to be highly descriptive, oriented to specific local political processes and did not provide operational conclusions (Dahl-Østergaard et al., 2005: 11; Thornton and Cox, 2005: 6, 22–3; Chhotray and Hulme, 2009: 45).

The history of the Drivers of Change approach indicates that its initial driving force was located at DFID headquarters, within the Governance Department, and that the method was soon left to the country offices. At the country level, particular DFID staff members turned out to be champions of the approach in later years. Yet, despite the fact that they found the analyses useful to get a better understanding of the local political economy, the approach did not provide them with solutions for the dilemmas they faced in their day-to-day work and played a limited role in the revision of country strategies (Dahl-Østergaard et al., 2005: 15–17). In the end, Drivers of Change analyses appear to have run up to the limitations of the practical nature of development work, where staff feel pressure to increase spending and work on programmes in the light of the Millennium Development Goals.

The lofty goals of understanding realities better may thus 'not be well aligned with donor incentives to demonstrate short term impact, respond to their own taxpayers and lobby groups, and to spend the allocated aid resources' (Dahl-Østergaard et al., 2005: 26–7). Moreover, for individual staff members

> internal, organisational incentives [supporting] continued development and implementation of DOC work ... are relatively weak [and require] more visible support from senior staff, as well as changes in human resource management systems, in order to demonstrate (through performance assessment, promotions and postings) that skills in political analysis, and country level knowledge, are valued and rewarded.
>
> (Dahl-Østergaard et al., 2005: 19)

The conclusion is that Drivers of Change has mainly contributed to raising the awareness of political-economic realities in partner countries staff among DFID country officers and country specialists at headquarters (Dahl-Østergaard et al., 2005: 7). In recent years, the approach seems to have been applied mostly at the sectoral level, and thereby seems to have largely lost its potential influence on general policy-making.

The Strategic Governance and Corruption Analysis

Dutch policy-making on development has been showing a commitment to principles of 'good governance' ever since the arrival of social-democrat Eveline Herfkens as Minister for Development Cooperation in 1998. Herfkens, who had previously served as Executive Director at the World Bank, changed the orientation of Dutch development assistance by embracing aid selectivity, in that a limited set of countries were chosen for Dutch bilateral development assistance on the basis of 'the presence of good policies and good governance in the recipient countries' (Minister for Development Cooperation, 1998: 2, translated from Dutch).

Subsequent Ministers for Development Cooperation (christian-democrat Agnes van Ardenne and social-democrat Bert Koenders) increased the number of Dutch partner countries from 22 to over 30, while maintaining a concern with governance in aid-recipient countries.[4] Koenders, in particular, showed great interest in the quality of governance in developing countries, as witnessed in a major speech on the modernisation of Dutch development assistance in November 2008: 'Good governance is a huge boost for development, and that is why I am investing in building the rule of law and well-functioning government' (Koenders, 2008: 9). In his own words, he was applying a 'more political conception of good governance' (Koenders, 2007: 9). His call for a political strategy for good governance was grounded in attention for the 'context' that influences the success of policies aimed at fighting corruption, strengthening the rule of law and building democracy (Koenders, 2007: 6).

The so-called SGACA, which had been conceived by the Directorate-General for International Cooperation at the Dutch Ministry of Foreign Affairs in 2006 and was introduced in 2007, resonated well with Koenders' views on governance. SGACA was introduced by the Human Rights, Good Governance and Humanitarian Aid Department (DMH)[5] with the clear aim of integrating the analysis with standard policy-making procedures at the Ministry. The instrument was given a role in the design of Multi-Annual Strategic Plans (MASPs) per embassy with the intention of enhancing the 'operational' value of the analyses.

The introduction of SGACA took place after a lengthy period of internal discussions at the Ministry about the proper way to integrate governance-oriented concerns into Dutch development policy, during which the need to understand 'informal' governance processes was expressed very clearly (cf. Harth and Waltmans, 2007; Waltmans, 2008). The main champion of SGACA was the Ministry of Foreign Affairs' DMH Department. After a period of rivalry with the Department for Effectiveness and Quality (DEK), the two departments agreed that their mutual involvement with 'good governance' would be solved by a division of labour: where DMH would deal with issues of 'legitimacy', DEK would be in charge of 'effectiveness'.[6] DEK, which had been the Ministry's primary responsible for the provision of macroeconomic (budget) support, for instance as part of debt relief, had developed the 'track record' instrument for ascertaining the degree to which partner countries would qualify for general or sectoral budget support.[7] DEK displayed a generally sceptical attitude towards the SGACA approach, as they felt that the results of political economy analyses, which zero in on accountability mechanisms and practices of corruption, could impact on the attitude in Parliament towards the provision of budget support.[8]

The starting point and central element of the SGACAs was the so-called Power and Change Analyses (PCAs), which would be a political economy assessment aiming to bring out what are the determinants, in state–society relationships, of countries' governance problems. According to the SGACA framework, the 'underlying assumption' of the analysis was 'that building more effective, accountable states and public institutions requires a political process of interaction between the state and (organised groups in) society' (Ministry of Foreign Affairs, 2008: 10).

The SGACAs' PCAs addressed, in a similar way as the Drivers of Change studies, three aspects of the political economy of aid-receiving developing countries: the 'foundational factors', the 'rules of the game' and the 'here and now' (the current context and main actors and stakeholders).[9] The approach envisaged that operational implications would be derived from the SGACAs during workshops organised at the embassies (Ministry of Foreign Affairs, 2008: 6–7). As it was put in the SGACA framework:

> The PCA can help with refining existing choices or making new ones, by enhancing understanding of context (the underlying causes of bad governance and weak development); and high-lighting opportunities and threats arising from that context that should inform all donor interventions.
>
> (Ministry of Foreign Affairs, 2008: 27)

The first of 29 completed SGACA exercises started from the assumption that the PCA would be a 'quick scan', on the basis of governance assessments made by the Dutch embassies (the so-called 'track records' – see above) and other available material, such as academic publications and policy-oriented reports. On the basis of the pilot phase, which took place in the second quarter of 2007, a decision was taken to increase the time allocated to the work of the international and local consultants in order to provide more solid analyses.[10]

Despite the increase of resources allocated to the analyses, interviews[11] with direct observers of the SGACA exercises indicate that the quality of the PCAs was highly variable. In certain cases, the limited expertise of the consultants was mentioned as a cause of poor quality, while in other cases the relative failure of SGACAs was ascribed to the lack of interest among embassy staff. Most observers agree that the decision by the Minister for Development Cooperation to bring the drafting of the MASPs for 2009–2012 forward had important negative impacts on the SGACA process. As fewer than half of all 29 SGACAs had been completed by the time the MASPs were finalised at the beginning of 2008, most SGACA reports failed to feed into decision-making on multi-annual programming.

The lack of support for the SGACA exercises seems, at least in part, due to a similar logic that was noted in the section on Drivers of Change above. The scepticism at the DEK is an expression of the common 'bureaucratic politics' that exists in any Ministry and that is related to the perceived threats emanating from projects undertaken by other Departments. In addition to this, regional Departments in the Ministry of Foreign Affairs expressed their fear that the analysis of the political-economic reality of partner countries would damage their relationships with governments.[12] Similar fears were present at

Dutch embassies in the partner countries, as they felt the threat of political fallout from reports on patronage and corruption on their budget support to country governments, and these added to the feelings of a general lack of ownership at the embassies. A good number of embassy staff saw the SGACA exercise as an imposition by the headquarters in The Hague, which interfered with their normal way of doing development business in the partner country. Passive resistance during the planning of SGACAs and reluctance to participate actively in the implementation of the political economy analyses were the main signs of the lack of ownership at embassy level. The SGACA end-of-project review summed up the embassies' attitude to the exercises by comparing them to a trip to the dentist: they were seen as 'something to be endured and ideally to be as short as possible' (ECORYS Nederland, 2009: 28). The outcome of bureaucratic quibbles at headquarters and lack of support throughout the organisation was also noted by one senior consultant, who made quite a damning statement about the exercise:

> Fundamentally, implementation was the main problem, as there were internal problems within the ministry, as well as problems in the relationship between Departments. Ministry staff basically had no idea as to how really address governance issues. People never got seriously down to analysing what type of changes would be needed. Apart from the Minister's commitment, there was no leadership within the organisation to implement SGACA and the governance programmes. The process was not just mismanaged, it was not managed at all.[13]

The SGACA process came to an end only little more than three years after its inception. The DMH had been considering an 'action plan' in order to bring the usefulness of 'political economy thinking' to the attention of embassy staff, but this idea was finally abandoned in early 2010. Instead of the action plan, a set of briefing papers on the salient components of the SGACA exercise was produced to inform staff at Dutch embassies and at the Ministry.[14] The fate of SGACA seems, therefore, rather similar to that of the Drivers of Change, as its main value is seen to derive from the contribution that political economy analysis has on the sensitivity of embassy staff to interests and power struggles in the partner countries.

Political economy analysis, policy reform and political risk

The World Bank has come a long way in its thinking about the political economy of governance practices. During the 1990s, the Bank was leading the introduction of notions of governance to the development discourse, in recognition of the failure of the purely macroeconomic focus of the 'Washington Consensus'. The World Bank's engagement with governance showed an attempt to avoid political aspects by arguing that 'governance may be relevant to the Bank's work if it is addressed in terms of having good order and discipline in the management of a country's resources' (World Bank 1991: 3).

The World Development Report 2002 was premised on the notion that markets are the central element of development: 'income from participating in the market is the key to boosting economic growth for nations and to reducing poverty for individuals' (World Bank, 2002a: 3). The main challenge in fighting poverty was almost reduced to a microeconomic issue: it would involve creating opportunities and incentives for poor people to make use of markets (cf. Fine, 2003: 14). 'Good governance' precepts would limit the role of the state to that of a regulator. The World Development Report 2002 distinguished four elements, in particular, as tasks of a well-governed state: the securing of property rights, regulation aimed at promoting competition, macroeconomic policies for stimulating market activity and the fight against corruption (World Bank, 2002a: 99).

In a self-assessment published in 2005, the World Bank embraced some significant conceptual and theoretical innovations that contained an implicit criticism of and distancing from its earlier apolitical, technocratic approach. Interestingly, the self-assessment argues:

> Perhaps the most important lesson of the 1990s is that technocratic responses to improve governance work only in very auspicious settings – where there is committed leadership, a broadly based coalition in support of reform, and sufficient capacity to carry the reform process forward. ... Meeting the challenge requires a good understanding of the political dimensions of reform, and, in particular, of how reform can be used to identify and build constituencies that are capable of sustaining the reform momentum.
>
> (World Bank, 2005: 298)

Although the report seemed to display much greater sensitivity to political dynamics than in the past, the 'guidelines' for policy reform as formulated by the Bank remained limited to the creation of incentives for economic actors, the pursuit of growth strategies and the creation of institutional conditions for a favourable investment climate (World Bank, 2005: 262–5).

More recent approaches presented by the World Bank appear to signal a change in orientation. In particular, a report of the Social Development Department (World Bank, 2008a) and a so-called 'good practice framework', published by the World Bank's Poverty Reduction and Economic Management (PREM) Network (Fritz et al., 2009) stand out as representatives of seemingly new thinking on political processes within the Bank. Given the interpretation of the overall orientation of the development community and the incentives inherent to their functioning, it is, however, doubtful whether the Bank's new ideas will produce more than 'the next "fix", limited to a narrow and fairly mechanistic kind of stakeholder analysis' (Unsworth, 2005: 8).

The Social Development Department's approach to the political economy of policy reform is based on Poverty and Social Impact Analysis in specific sectors, such as agriculture and water. The 'political economy of reform' revolves around three distinctive elements: the reform context, the reform arena and the reform process (World Bank, 2008a: 10). The reform context relates to the socio-economic, political, cultural and historical institutions that impact on reform. The reform arena includes societal 'rules of the game', stakeholders and their interests. The reform process refers to 'information flows, voice and public debate' that determine who sets the agenda for reform and how proposed policy changes are communicated (World Bank, 2008a: 11–13). Together, the three elements set an 'action framework' that comprises elements such as: the timing and sequencing of reforms, analysis of the 'demand and supply' of reform in order to build coalitions for change, and partnership and public communication strategies (World Bank, 2008a: 11, 43–50). The ultimate aim of the political economy of policy reform appears to assess 'the most significant political economy and political risks to policy reform'. By gaining knowledge on how political economy and political 'variables' impact on the outcome of reform processes, development agencies should increase their options for influencing the political-economic risks and opportunities (World Bank, 2008a: 16).

In line with the political economy of policy reform, the PREM Network's 'problem-driven governance and political economy analysis' is also set up in order to enhance the effectiveness of World Bank interventions (Fritz et al., 2009: vii). The Bank, so much is clear from the framework, stresses the instrumental nature of its approach, as governance and political economy analysis

> can help to anticipate and manage risks – including risks of reform failure, of Bank-supported reforms triggering unintended negative consequences, as well as potential reputational risks. It can also assist in transmitting important knowledge about institutions and stakeholders more quickly and effectively to staff newly joining a country or other operational team.
>
> (Fritz et al., 2009: 1)

Consistent with most other approaches, 'problem-driven governance and political economy analysis' distinguishes three 'clusters of drivers': structures, institutions and actors or stakeholders (Fritz et al., 2009: 40–4). Together, these clusters impact on political and public sector action and, ultimately, on the outcomes of policies, such as growth, poverty reduction and provision of public goods.

The problem-driven nature of the approach is linked to its focus on specific problems or issues that appear to be spurred by particular 'governance and political economy weaknesses'. On the basis of the identification of such problems, the approach would proceed to the second 'layer' of uncovering the institutional and governance arrangements in society and 'drill down' to the third 'layer' where the three mentioned clusters of political economy drivers represent obstacles to change, or opportunities for reform (Fritz et al., 2009: 7). The bottom line of the problem-driven approach is that reform proposals should be 'feasible'. Rather than advocating all encompassing governance reform, 'good enough governance' should be the focus of development agencies (Fritz et al., 2009: 12).

Although the framework alludes to 'country-level analysis', specific sectors and policy themes receive most attention (Fritz et al., 2009: 23). It is at this level that the framework seems to see the best opportunities for the application of governance and political economy analysis. In particular, the authors of the framework suggest three options. In the first place, analyses would inform World Bank staff teams how to adjust strategies and operations to existing opportunities for change. Further, such analyses would enhance and broaden the policy dialogue with country governments. Finally, findings of the governance and political economy analyses would point out opportunities for supporting change proactively (Fritz et al., 2009: 17–21).

On the basis of the two political economy approaches propagated in World Bank circles, one is led to conclude that the changes to the Bank's approach, if any, have taken largely an instrumental character. Unsworth's (2005: 8) expectation that a predominantly 'mechanistic kind of stakeholder analysis' would prevail has, so far, not been falsified. The above discussion has made clear that knowledge about the political economy of borrowing countries is considered relevant mostly for judging what are the main limits to implementing policy reform, and how political risks can be minimised. The World Bank's earlier plea, in the stock-taking exercise of 2005 (quoted above), that more attention should be paid to the 'political dimensions of reform' seems to have had only limited impact on its day-to-day operations. The World Bank's operations in the developing world through the International Development Association (IDA) have remained 'business as usual'. It remains to be seen whether 'political economy' will change Bank practices in the future.

The Bank's application of the Country Policy and Institutional Assessment (CPIA) may illustrate the limited impact that political economy analysis has had so far on the Bank's policy on lending to developing countries. The CPIA, which was introduced at the end of the 1990s in order to render IDA allocations more sensitive to recipient countries' reform of policies and governance, has been one of the most fiercely criticised instruments in international development financing.[15] Much of the criticism of the instrument centres on its neo-liberal, market-oriented bias. Despite a recent revision of the CPIA methodology, assessments of country performance in the 2008–2011 period are being determined, for about two-thirds, by a governance-related cluster of five measures (International Development Association, 2008: 43–5).[16] These measures are:

- property rights and rule-based governance;
- quality of budgetary and financial management;
- efficiency of revenue mobilisation;
- quality of public administration; and
- transparency, accountability and corruption in the public sector.

Thus, the emphasis of IDA's governance assessments continues to be on impediments for private sector activity, on public sector management in relation to public finance, taxation and service delivery, and on checks on government. There are no signs that the allocation of loans to developing countries has become less performance-based and less reliant on the technocratic and market-oriented CPIA. Further, it is not clear how the change in thinking on political economy analysis is reflected in actual lending practices, nor how the awareness of political dimensions of reform is featured into projects and programmes aimed at strengthening governance in developing countries. On the basis of information that is available at the time of writing, the changes advocated in the two new political economy frameworks seem to have little impact on day-to-day World Bank policy practices.

Conclusion

This chapter's discussion of various approaches to political economy analysis indicates that such instruments do not sit very comfortably among the range of tasks undertaken by development agencies. The unease of development agencies does not seem to derive from the objectives of this type of analysis – which are generally understood and endorsed, at least at the level of policy-makers at headquarters – but is a consequence of the way in which the agencies define their own tasks, and of the internal operation that is a result of the structure of their organisational interests.

Three examples (the UK's Drivers of Change, the Dutch Strategic Governance and Corruption Analysis and the World Bank's approaches to political economy analysis) have been discussed in this chapter. Despite their pretensions the former two approaches did not produce many concrete results in terms of day-to-day policy-making. The Drivers of Change and the SGACA in the end seemed mainly to be tools for enhancing the understanding among embassy or country office staff of the political-economic realities in the countries they are posted to. Vagueness of the methodologies appears to have been a factor contributing to the limited use of the approaches, as was the lack of operational embedding. The launching by the World Bank of a political economy framework has not appeared to have changed dramatically the way the Bank is dealing with governance issues. Its sectoral application of political economy analysis seems to be 'inward-looking', in that it aims to limit the risk of reform failure and reputational risk. The increased attention to political aspects of governance, which dates back at least to a major self-assessment published in 2005, has not impacted on the way the Bank deals with lending to developing countries, as the IDA's main diagnostic tool remains biased to technocratic and market-oriented performance indicators.

The examples illustrate that development agencies have many traits of an epistemic community: their staff have a more or less common outlook on the world and share a set of values and norms related to poverty reduction and advancing development in countries of the global South. This outlook leads to a rather instrumental approach to development programmes and projects, which tends to pay little attention to political struggles and power relations and defines governance in predominantly apolitical terms. Staff are motivated, in the first place, by 'doing development' in a professional way, which implies choosing the best instruments for obtaining a maximum of results.

In addition to their shared norms and values, the structure of incentives within donor agencies is an important determinant of the outlook of development professionals on the issue of politics. For staff, 'doing development' implies managing and implementing programmes and projects, and disbursing funds to partner organisations – predominantly governments, but also others – in order to obtain results. The depoliticised understanding of development is instrumental for development professionals, as this helps them focus on the key elements of their work, without being 'distracted' by the potential conflicts of interest among their partners and the power implications of development processes.

The technocratic and apolitical framing of governance will not, of course, surprise readers of the work of well-known authors such as James Ferguson and John Harriss. Ferguson (1990), who focused on the implementation of development policies in Lesotho, and Harriss (2001), who analysed the usage of 'social capital' by the World Bank, pointed out already long ago that the international development community is operating as an 'anti-politics machine'. More recently, Sue Unsworth (2009), the former Chief Governance Advisor at the UK's DFID, argued that donor agencies find it inherently 'hard to come to terms with politics'.

The tension between the fundamentally depoliticised understanding of governance and the call for political sensitivity seems to be one of the inherent characteristics of 'Aidland' (Apthorpe, quoted by Eyben, 2007: 22). Those responsible for policy-making on development assistance, usually at headquarters, generally recognise the need for more fundamental, political or political economy, analysis of development reality behind the 'façade' of formal political institutions. People out 'in the field', however, will generally understand that interests are part of the development process, but tend to set the priorities for their own day-to-day activities differently under the influence of the incentives that have been discussed above. Although the current framework of international development seems to require a 'political understanding of aid delivery' by development agencies (de Haan and Everest-Phillips, 2007: 15), it is unlikely that the persistent emphasis on 'doing development' will give way to a more profound engagement with politics. The irony is that as long as development practice is seen as an expert activity, not an act of politics, the development 'industry' will continue to operate as the 'anti-politics machine' that it has always been (Ferguson, 1990).

4
Development as Collective Action Problems

Introduction

The discussion of various attempts at engaging with political economy analysis by development agencies in the previous chapter showed that such agencies have difficulty in engaging with politics, as a consequence of the understanding they have of their work, as well as their own institutional political-economic realities. This chapter turns to further attempts to operationalise political economy analysis within the broader development community and particularly to the idea that development can be understood as a set of collective action problems, wherein political action is necessary to obtain 'development' as a public good so the whole of society is made better off.

Our criticism of this understanding of development is advanced in two parts. First, we focus on recent strategies to increase aid effectiveness by supporting progressive social forces to drive reform, particularly through 'demand for good governance' and greater social accountability. The demand for good governance approach was touted as a logical next political step by the donor agencies involved, however, we show how and why this approach in fact pays little heed to actual political (and even administrative) processes by positively disdaining forms of political engagement that involve contestation over collective futures. This newer strand of development policy was not discussed alongside the political economy approaches in the previous chapter, because 'demand for good governance' is an explicit attempt to *engage with* politics rather than avoid it, or turn it into a factor in a risk calculus. We are nevertheless critical of the demand for good governance approach's portrayal of politics as an instrument to resolve collective action obstacles to development.

Second, the chapter discusses how the project to help donors work-politically is sustained by a *political economy community* of development professionals, consultants and academics – often with funding links to donor agencies but publishing independently through policy papers and/or academic journals.[1] This 'small but influential community working in or around' the aid industry does 'not constitute a unified movement', but shares a number of distinguishing orientations and themes, sufficient to class it as a community (Carothers and de Gramont, 2013: 160). In many respects, these shared orientations and themes – the attention given to political agency and institutional reform in particular – are a logical consequence of the community's primary intention to apply political analysis to the achievement of reform.

Our concern is that, largely, the approaches of this political economy community are underpinned by liberal conceptions of state and society, such that the political problem in development terms is how to resolve the *dysfunctionality* of the conflicts of interest which stand in way of the realisation of the whole of society's common interest in collective goods, such as economic growth, infrastructure, health and so on. Also, because political processes are a major factor in policy choices and their consequences, the long-term answer is still thought to lie in changing how political institutions operate so as to lock in the right processes for good, developmental outcomes (Batley et al., 2012: 135). The political economy community does not consider these collective goods should be prescribed by technical experts, as they are determined by domestic political processes. Nevertheless, it leans to the association of power with authority, and its legitimate use or function 'to mobilise commitments or obligations for effective collective action', as against power in relation to structural conflicts of interest (Hyden, 2008: 262).[2]

Demand-side reform

Starting in the late 1990s, various World Bank reports engaged with the need to 'bring the state closer to the people' – notably through enhancing 'user participation' in service delivery and 'giving people a voice' to express their 'concerns' about such services (World Bank, 1997). By 2001, the Bank had acknowledged that the issue of state responsiveness is 'intrinsically political and requires active collaboration among poor people, the middle class, and other groups in society' (World Bank, 2001: 7). Thereafter, in the 2004 World Development Report, *Making Services Work for the Poor*, and the *Governance and Anti-Corruption Strategy* approved in 2007, there was further scaling-up of the argument for 'multi-stakeholder engagement', especially via social accountability mechanisms – this included citizens' report cards, public expenditure tracking surveys, participatory budgeting and so on – specifically to enhance information flows and societal oversight of government processes. In this, the poor were portrayed as combining two subjectivities – that of client and that of citizen. In their role as 'client' the poor were seen as consumers of existing public services, such as health and education, much in the same way as they were looked upon as buyers of individual goods, such as rice and chicken, in the market place (World Bank, 2004: 6). However, where services were perceived as substandard or non-existent, the poor should use their roles as 'citizens' to lobby the government to in turn discipline the service provider. This chain of accountability was referred to by the Bank as the 'long route' – a route which frequently breaks down because there are rather more steps in the process.

The conception of accountability that was adopted in these and similar World Bank publications is decidedly liberal and contractual: state actors have obligations to clients and citizens, but such obligations derive from – and are therefore restricted to – their proper role as public officials and not from their democratic duty to respect the people's sovereign authority and collective will (Rodan and Hughes, 2012). As David Williams and Tom Young (1994: 93–4) explain, in relation to proper governance, liberalism is normally assumed to separate the 'right' (in the sense of proper rules and procedures) from the 'good' (in the sense of the desired outcomes) in order to uphold individual freedoms. Accordingly, liberals are known to advocate that 'the State should be a neutral framework within which competing conceptions of the good can be equally pursued'. However, Williams and Young point out this distinction is in fact only sustainable if liberal comprehensions of state and society are accepted and that, in the case of the World Bank, it is clear its 'technical' reforms are shaped by 'a prior conception of the good' (1994: 94). Hence, the development goal of the 'effective state' may be cast as neutrally right, but in truth it embodies the good of a market economy which is locked in through property rights and contracts (see World Bank, 2007b).

On this basis, in policy terms state actors' obligations to address citizens' demands are limited to this prior notion of the good and, conversely, citizens' demands are conceived of as rebalancing the political incentives for state actors to do the proper thing. Not only does the World Bank's social accountability framework thus assume that citizens have an unambiguous preference for good governance and effective service delivery (Booth, 2012): it goes further in prescribing what are acceptable political goals and actions, worthy of donors' attention and support. As a result, the vaunted 'empowerment' of citizens is considered to be established by rather limited modes of engagement, such as consultation or complaint mechanisms over a restricted list of government service functions.

Taking forward the views developed by the World Bank, the Australian Agency for International Development (AusAID), in its major programme *Building Demand for Better Governance*, defined demand for good governance in terms of 'partnerships' and therefore 'collaborative rather than oppositional relationships with government' (2007: 13). The call for partnerships was

> based on an understanding that calls for better governance and increased accountability are not dependent on a blunt oppositional stance, but can be based on partnership approaches that increase participation and openness in areas of mutual benefit, between citizens, key institutions in the enabling environment and states.
>
> (AusAID, 2007: 2)

In taking this approach, AusAID runs the risk of imposing forms of collaboration that disguise and marginalise conflict, rather than allowing it political expression. Indeed, this approach narrows the scope of acceptable forms of opposition to well within the rather broad limits envisaged by classical liberalism as, eliminated from the outset is the idea of fundamental conflicts of interest emerging in the course of development.

Nevertheless, other development agencies' interest in supporting social accountability mechanisms and civil society organisations has helped to foster valuable policy-linked research into 'the new politics of inclusion' and active citizenship (Houtzager and Moore, 2003; Benequista and Gaventa, 2011). The findings of this research have challenged the 'supply and demand' conception of politics, and the dualism of state and civil society which underpin it, in favour of a focus on the interactions between state and societal actors (also Fox, 2007; Centre for the Future State, 2010: 10). Significantly, this saw an appreciable shift in terminology towards more 'talk of collective actors, coalitions, and institutions' (Houtzager, 2003: 13).

The Department for International Development (DFID) was an important funder of this and similar critical research. In *The Politics of Poverty: Elites, Citizens and States*, the development of citizens as actors was regarded as requiring the forging of 'broad coalitions ... who also link to and build alliances with reformers in the state' to promote change through 'contention and contestation – both inherent in how they are framed and in how they are fought' (DFID, 2010: 55). In regards to contentious coalitions as 'drivers of change', DFID thus explicitly challenged 'approaches to participation and civic engagement, which reduce such processes to technical solutions, or to notions of and process of "national ownership" achieved through non-contentious consultation and dialogue – but which veil vast chasms of differences in power and interests' (2010: 55). Moreover, DFID regarded the mere provision of state-sponsored space for participation as insufficient to challenge such inequalities: the mobilisation of 'broad-based coalitions' on their own terms would be required (2010: 64), and this should apply to ex-ante contention over policy as well as ex-post contention over the quality of services delivered (2010: 67). This led DFID to an understanding of development which requires collective action to challenge dominant power relations.

However, even in DFID's relatively radical formulations we see certain restrictions imposed. First, DFID persisted in viewing collective action as an instrument or means for 'institutional fixing' rather than as an end in itself, in terms of challenging power relations in society. 'Development' remained a project to be 'delivered' rather than constructed through political action. Although DFID also flagged the need for broad-based coalitions to undertake collective action, these were regarded in terms of securing policy change rather than as fundamental to the political settlement itself. We find a similar approach to be ongoing in the liberal strand of the political economy community.[3]

Another line of criticism of the 'demand-side' approach also feeds into the recent attention to collective action as problem-solving. Booth argues that the 'demand-side' approach ignores the multiple accountabilities, incentives and pressures that political actors experience in relation to their sources and power in decision-making

(Booth, 2012: 35). In administrative terms alone, policy implementation and service delivery invariably require cross- and intra-departmental coordination, in which case, 'ill-defined mandates or overlapping jurisdictions' create 'confused responsibilities' – particularly when institutions are weak (Booth, 2012: 36). Hence, lines of accountability are not simple or clean, even in the 'short route' between service providers and service users, especially when such services are under development or in a poor state.

To sum up, Carothers and de Gramont (2013: 140) make the important observation that issues which donors and donor-supported groups 'treat as objectively desirable reform items are in fact parts of larger political agendas'. To quote them:

> The focus on putatively universal principles such as inclusiveness and accountability hides the reality of basic ideological choice and contest. Societal actors necessarily operate in an environment of competition and conflict without clear lines between what is 'reform' and what is 'anti-reform' and in which there is no simple duality of citizens versus the state. … Development agencies frequently lack understanding of how their agendas fit into these domestic political debates and power struggles and are reluctant to acknowledge the contested nature of their goals.

The above discussion illustrates that there has been serious criticism of the 'demand-side' approach voiced by the political economy community. In the next section, we go on to argue that the liberal pluralist strand of this community nevertheless shares the understanding of development as a public good from which everyone benefits in the end. We show that it does take politics more seriously by seeking to understand actual processes of reform – or how change actually happens (Williams et al., 2011: S29). Not unreasonably, they argue that change happens through collective action, but they then link this almost exclusively to the resolution of collective action *problems* – which feature in rational choice institutionalist understandings of politics and development.

Political agency

Members of the political economy community start from the assumption that development outcomes are determined by political processes.

Most importantly, politics is viewed positively as providing 'ways forward' for reform rather than simply obstacles in its way (Centre for the Future State, 2010: 6). Because the community is concerned to use political economy insights to promote change, there tends to be a strong and distinctive focus on the role of political agency. In structure and agency debates regarding causation in the social sciences, 'agency' usually denotes a degree of 'free will, choice or autonomy' – and hence indeterminacy and contingency – in making history, in contrast with the idea that historical outcomes are relatively fixed and predictable as they arise directly from systemic features and tendencies (Hay, 2002: 93–6).

Accordingly, for the political economy community a focus on agency is a corrective to the perceived overemphasis on structure and institutions in development policy and literature – the 'dismal science of constraints' as some have labelled it (Duncan and Williams, 2012: 145; also Fabella, 2011; Leftwich, 2011: 2–3). However, agency is not simply a matter of voluntarism. In a paper produced for the Developmental Leadership Program (DLP), Adrian Leftwich defines political agency as 'all the activities of conflict, negotiation and compromise' that go towards 'mobilising people and resources in support of a particular goal or goals' (Leftwich, 2011: 1–2).[4] In other words, according to this definition, political agency encompasses all aspects of civic contestation which fall short of outright violence and war. In this understanding, context matters since in a very real sense political agency entails 'working the system': because all political processes are structured, structures are the medium of agency and not its antonym (Hay, 2002; Leftwich, 2011).

In seeking to apply political analysis to the achievement of better development outcomes, understandably the political economy community is interested to focus on the 'room to manoeuver' that is created in and through political processes. This is something Merilee Grindle (2004a) earlier highlighted in her classic study of the politics of education reform in Latin America (see Booth and Golooba-Mutebi, 2009; Leftwich, 2011; Duncan and Williams, 2012). To quote Grindle: 'reform initiatives need to be viewed as dynamic political processes that unfold over time, as complex chains of decisions subject to the interaction of reform advocates and opponents in particular institutional contexts that are sometimes subject to alteration' (2004a: 15). This matches the DLP's conception of political agency. However, in developing country contexts, political agency is said to be especially important in shaping developing outcomes because there is generally a dearth of strong institutions and governance systems (Leftwich and Hogg, 2007: 4; Centre for the Future State, 2010). Under these circumstances, informal mechanisms play a prominent role, as does by implication the political priorities of elites (see McCourt, 2003).

This conception of political agency differs from the ontology of agency and structure in rational choice institutionalism in that it gives more credence to agency. Rational choice theory holds the individual to be 'primary and given', consequently it is the individual's *conduct*, not their *preferences*, that is perceived to be shaped by the institutional setting. In this 'calculus approach', institutions affect individuals' conduct 'by altering the expectations an actor has about the actions that others are likely to take in response to, or simultaneously with, his [sic] own action' (Hall and Taylor, 1996: 939). As Colin Hay (2002: 53) observes, for rationalists, structure or context is therefore everything in human conduct. Because all people are motivated to selfishly maximise their own welfare, their conduct in seeking to realise this goal is only varied by the milieu in which this occurs. So long as they continue to act in a rational fashion, individuals' actions in a particular setting will be predictable and, importantly, subject to manipulation through changes to that setting. There is thus no room in rational choice approaches for indeterminacy and sociological diversity in agency. For the political economy community, by contrast, agency and the attendant factors of motivation and commitment are important determinants of change. Yet, these are not equated with 'political will' – as a purely mental phenomenon – rather they are thought to be much more 'a function of the way in which political processes work' (Leftwich, 2007: 26, also Melo et al., 2012: 178–82).

The political economy community's conception of agency is also more relational than that of rational choice approaches, in that it takes account of collective action beyond the aggregation of individual conduct. However, this collective action is linked again to the perceived need to resolve collective action problems for development. This is seen in the DLP's approach to 'coalitions'. For Leftwich, coalitions are key to 'overcoming pervasive collective action problems *that are at the core of all politics*, especially the politics of development' (2012: 6–7, emphasis added). Defined as 'individuals, groups or organizations that come together to achieve social, political and economic goals they would not be able to achieve on their own' (Leftwich, 2012: 5; also Leftwich and Hogg, 2007: 5), coalitions are thus seen to entail the forms of joint action required to address the conflicts of interest which stand in the way of positive development outcomes for all.

In rational choice political economy, collective action problems necessarily arise because, unless they are otherwise forced or stimulated to do so, 'self-interested individuals will not act to achieve their common or group interest' (Olson, 1965: 2; Gibson et al., 2005). Collective action *problems* need *collective action* solutions in the limited sense of individuals coming together to adjust their conduct through collaboration and/or to establish the more permanent institutions to habituate appropriate behaviours over the longer term. In the absence of strong institutions in developing counties, the initial challenge is how to ensure that 'the members of the same community work together to attain a collective goal that benefits all' (Fabella, 2011: 236). Or, put another way, the key question is thought to be: 'How does a society make collective policy decisions that affect it as a whole, given conflicting interests?' (Tolentino, 2010: 3).

For the DLP and some others in the political economy community, the answer to this question rests in the formation and support for developmental coalitions. Coalitions are a key reform mechanism because they enable coordinated action across a range of interests and perspectives, and they are more flexible and task-oriented than organisations. Put simply:

> Coalitions facilitate dialogue: representatives of opposing coalitions may be brought together to discuss the reforms and achieve mutually acceptable solutions. Dialogue among coalitions may also produce mutually supported ideas for transition mechanisms and assistance for those who lose from the reforms.
>
> (Tolentino, 2010: 13)

In this instance, the conception of politics is more pluralist than rational choice as collective action problems are seen to arise from conflicts of interest operating at sectional and group levels, as well as individual levels (Leftwich, 2012: 7). But when, in other parts of the political economy community, there is a stronger focus on the commitment and conduct of elites, we see context again becomes the dynamic element in development politics. For example, Gareth

Williams et al. (2011) and Lindsay Whitfield and Ole Therkildsen (2011) stress the need to consider how state and private sector actors' interactions are shaped by elite's political calculations that relate to their principal interest in power and consequent need to sustain supportive coalitions.

So, whilst there is some variation in the political economy community's understandings of the relative importance of agency versus context, and therefore the need for collective action versus changes to incentive structures, there is a high degree of convergence over the idea that development politics is about the resolution of collective action problems. When it is foregrounded, collective action is limited to ways of working together to find the solutions to shared welfare obstacles which cannot be addressed through independent action. It is therefore how the nature of the development problem is understood that makes coalition building so crucial in this approach. This view of collective action is different from that which refers to the means of garnering power through collective association and mass actions to achieve strength in numbers – our preferred understanding from a structural political economy perspective.[5]

Also, whilst not ignoring power, for the political economy community power is much more associated with authority and how that is exercised in relation to collective goals. Hence, there is among representatives of the community a strong emphasis on the need to build 'effective, accountable public authority' that 'can undertake core governance functions' (Centre for the Future State, 2010: 7–9). The term public authority does not refer simply to formal institutions of the state as the view is: 'States are not the only sources of public authority. In most poor countries the boundaries between "state" and "society" are unclear, and the task of organising collective action to create public goods may be shared between a great variety of state and non-state actors' (Centre for the Future State, 2010: 9–10). Nevertheless, for the political economy community, the *solution* to collective action problems lies clearly in institution building.

Institutionalisation is considered a transformative political process as it works through disciplining individuals and social groups to interact and behave within acceptable rules and norms. The institutionalised regime becomes 'the only game in town' and all major social forces cease trying to overthrow the regime but instead seek to use it to promote their interests and causes. Collective action problems are ultimately solved through appropriate institutions that can provide predictability, trust and so on (Williams et al., 2011).

> These problems require institutional solutions that could be achieved, at least in part, if those involved were able to devise, agree and enforce an institutional arrangement (a set of rules) that would require each of them to restrain in some degree their immediate and short-term pursuit of self-interest so that they would all be better off in the medium term.
>
> (Leftwich, 2012: 7)

This understanding of institutions is derived from liberal ideas of a plural society – a society in which a range of ad hoc and fairly fluid interest groups contend on a reasonably level playing field to influence day-to-day policy decisions. Institutionalisation is relatively easy in such a society because the benefits of institutions are obvious in this context: they provide predictability, justice and opportunities for all.

As we have seen, in rejecting strictly technical solutions, the political economy community does see good development outcomes as situational and arising out of local processes. Whilst disagreeing with the idea that development entails the application of some variant of 'international best practice', they do nevertheless hold to the view that there is a common good and that this is achieved through the right institutions to deliver collective goods. Goran Hyden (2008: 262) notes the distinction in political science between power 'used in a constructive fashion to achieve collective ends' ('power to') and power 'as manifesting itself in conflicts of interest' ('power over') and its relevance for aid effectiveness modalities. What is striking in interpretations of development as a collective action problem is that they do not perceive a problem around material and ideological conflicts *over* the nature of the public good because, fundamentally, the interests undermining the collective welfare are dismissed as objectively dysfunctional. In this way, the political economy community shares with the rest of the aid industry the idea that the primary political challenge is to 'mobilise commitments' by supporting the 'power to' of progressive actors; but this ignores or sidelines the structural dynamics in 'power over' (Hyden, 2008: 263).

However, there are exceptions. Recent writing on 'political settlements' in the political economy community is apparently an exception to the dominant collective goods orientation to development. This framework clearly understands institutions (and the state) are an outcome of power relations and the site of contestation (Di John and Putzel, 2009; Khan, 2010; Parks and Cole, 2010). It rejects the conception of institutions as incentive structures in favour of a more historical approach that argues 'institutions incorporate distributional advantages in line with the reigning political settlement' (Di John and Putzel, 2009: 8). Accordingly, these authors are much less sanguine about the role of institutions and their reform in development processes, on the basis that elite *power* generally trumps over 'rules' (Parks and Cole, 2010: 9). Hence, it is asserted, significant change happens only when there is a change in the elite's 'common understanding of how power is organized and exercised' (Park and Cole, 2010: 12). This steers away from the mainstream, liberal pluralist understanding of state and society, but remains focused on elites and the idea donor agencies have some capacity to intervene in political settlements to make them more inclusive.

Our notion of structural political economy, which is developed more in the next chapter, takes as its starting point the existence of a fundamentally unequal society formed of dominant and subordinate groups. This approach suggests that institutionalisation, while often reducing the level of violence, does not necessarily increase opportunities for the poor – consequently, habituating the poor to an institutional order that does not serve them particularly well is likely to be difficult. Indeed, institutionalisation may be more effective than outright repression as a means of suppressing demands for fundamental redistributions of power and resources in favour of the poor. Institutions, in our model, do not merely consist of more or less effective market regulation or key structures affecting individuals' actions. They are, rather, contingent features of the social and political order that reflect the power relations inherent in that order and operate to promote their long-term stability and the long-term ascendancy of dominant forces within them (Poulantzas, 1978; Jessop, 2002).

Discussions on working politically

Let us see then how the theoretical underpinnings of the political economy community are translated into recommendations for working politically. These fall into two main categories. The first involves 'identifying and leveraging influential partners with genuine interest in reform' (Tolentino, 2010: 12). This entails some form of support and encouragement for the progressive forces already present. In the second, the emphasis is more concertedly on the need to change incentive structures to shift elite interests, to have them commit to reform (Batley et al., 2012).

Developmental leadership

Consistent with a strong concern with public authority, the political economy community tends to focus on power-holders or 'elites'. Elites are 'a distinct group within a society which enjoys privileged status and exercises decisive control over the organization of society'. This does not require that the actors be either wealthy or members of the ruling class, but it does suggest that they have a measurable impact on development outcomes (Amsden et al., 2009). The developmental challenge is how to strengthen reform-oriented elites politically, so they better able to act in the public good.

The hunt for champions of reform is not new. In Southeast Asia in the 1970s and 1980s, donors' archetypal reformers were the technocrats: highly trained economists embedded in the national bureaucracy. Often such technocrats had been trained in the same institutions and were all speaking the language of economic liberalization. In the technocrats, donors found dedicated supporters of their policy agendas. Critically, however, the technocrats tended to lack the political clout to ensure policy adoption and implementation. In the Philippines under Marcos, technocrats in key ministries of finance and economic planning were influential in policy and planning and played a critical role in attracting foreign loans. Nevertheless, there was 'a big difference between influence in agenda-setting and in actual programme implementation' (Montes, 1989: 80). The paradox was that external funds in large part sustained the crony capitalism that benefited the real political power-holders (Hutchcroft, 1991).

Technocrats were important in an era in which development agencies considered anti-market policies were the main problem (Fabella, 2011: 225). Hence, in their staunch support for neoliberal policy prescriptions, technocrats were donors' ideal reformers. The political economy community continues to look for dedicated reformers, but also for those capable of providing local solutions to developmental problems through political processes. An example of this line of thinking can be found in The Asia Foundation publication on economic policy reform in the Philippines, where the focus is on 'development entrepreneurs'. Development entrepreneurs are defined as 'human actors who have the cognitive and emotional make-up – engendered either by nature or nurture – that leads them to pursue the greater social good through institutional change' and are 'willing to strategically engage ... in the murky world of political networking and bargaining' to that end (Faustino and Fabella, 2011: 261, *emphasis added*).

Developmental leaders are similar. Leaders are considered to be *developmental* – rather than predatory – when they embrace some notion of the collective good. As put by Leftwich and Hogg (2007:6), developmental leaders manage to 'reach beyond their immediate interests to a wider encompassing interest'. But such leaders are not only dedicated to reform, they importantly as well have the 'education, skills and experience that will enable them to devise and agree the rules of the game (institutions) that will organize and mediate the relationships between private interests and public goods so as to benefit all through growth and social development' (Leftwich and Hogg, 2007: 6). In short, developmental leaders have distinctive political capabilities and leadership is political itself: 'a process that involves the fostering and use of networks and the formation of coalitions as a means of overcoming the many collective action problems that define the challenges of development' (Lyne de Ver and Kennedy, 2011: 43; also Leftwich and Hogg, 2007; Leftwich and Wheeler, 2011). As such, leadership is a 'shared process between leaders and others' and not 'an individual trait' (Lyne de Ver and Kennedy, 2011: v). This is not the sort of heroic, 'transformational leadership' that Robert Rotberg (2012) identifies. For Rotberg, the transformational leader is the great, enlightened individual possessing the personal qualities to make a difference. They have the right 'motives and purposes' – political will – so 'are able more than others override structural constraints and to act largely autonomously' (2012: 10–11). In his view, leaders create followers not coalitions, and their genius is in ensuring that followers remain loyal.

According to this approach, working politically with developmental reformers is predominantly about donors offering a range of supporting roles (Faustino and Fabella, 2011: 263). These go well beyond the conventional idea of 'partnership' (see Chapter 7) to entail 'investing in processes to support the formation and effectiveness of developmental coalitions ... by enhancing not just technical skills (the conventional domain of capacity building) but also the political capacity of organizations in areas such as negotiation, advocacy, communication and the generation of constructive policy options' (Leftwich, 2011: 6). The Developmental Leadership Program (DLP), for example has encouraged case study research into ways of working politically, at national, sector or issue levels that are feasible for donors to consider (see Leftwich and Wheeler, 2011).

Incentives

In circumstances where power-holders are not developmental but predatory, the political economy community is concerned with the incentives that shape elite political conduct and how these might be changed. In this view it is vital that 'we should understand policy choices and implementation by looking at the incentives produced by the formal and informal political institutions characterizing the distribution and organization of political power in a specific country' (Whitfield and Therkildsen, 2011: 15). Hence, Alex Duncan and Gareth Williams (2012: 136) advocate 'looking creatively for ways to promote change that shifts political incentives in a pro-developmental direction'. The idea is to reconcile or align the interests of power-holders towards public good reform through changes to the incentives they are responding to (McCourt, 2003).

The challenge Williams et al. (2011) outline for donors and donor governments is how they might re-shape political leaders' incentives arising from factors such as these: the structure of the economy; government revenue sources; the nature and extent of political competition; and state-business relations. Suggestions include: appropriate trade agreements; transparency and accountability standards; action on money laundering (Williams et al., 2011: S44–S50). Similarly, Whitfield and Therkildsen (2011: 19) have emphasised the importance of structural and institutional contexts in shaping the main features of ruling coalitions. In particular, they point at the vulnerability of the ruling elite, this group's degree of fragmentation and it financial bases. Ultimately, in their view however, the success of the claim to power by the ruling elites depends on their ability to build and maintain coalitions:

Ruling elites want to stay in power, and staying in power requires building and maintaining a political organization, or what we call a ruling coalition. Consequently, ruling elites make policy decisions with an eye toward sustaining coalitions or persuading opposition members to change their stances.

(Whitfield and Therkildsen, 2011: 14)

The political economy community is concerned with incentives as inducements to action on needed reforms. However, it is often assumed to be political leaders' *calculations* with respect to their own advantage that matter; it is how leaders act on their impulse to retain power that is primary (see Whitfield and Therkildsen, 2011: 15). We agree instead with Sam Hickey (2012: 1244) on the need for 'sharper understandings of the incentives to which political elites respond, which go beyond straight forward calculations of personal or electoral gain to the role of ideology and beliefs'. In this and similar interpretations, ideological interpretations of the causes of poverty and who is considered responsible for addressing these are vital elements of the explanation of why elites support (or not) proposals aimed at poverty reduction (Hickey, 2012: 1238). This ideological dimension is largely missing from the political economy community's discussions of working politically because they hold to view that development is a public good, rather than continuously contested.

Conclusion

We started this chapter by emphasising that an important current within contemporary development thinking operates from the position that political processes are a key determinant of development outcomes. Accordingly, within the political economy community, politics is accepted as a fact of life, both immutable and necessary. However, in so far as the community's political analysis is applied to the goal of reform, politics is linked to problem solving, particularly in relation to collective action or social steering. And the focus tends to be on institutional rather than structural forms of power (Hickey, 2009: 146).

Our criticism of the argument on the public goods character of development is supported by various insights on the development process. In the first place, the very nature of development makes it into a process with political overtones. Development implies an intervention into socio-economic realities and relations. As it requires a change of the status quo, certain social groups will feel that their interests are being threatened. Thus, because of the deeply entrenched nature of many interests, it is highly unlikely that easy collective action solutions can be found for the problems emanating from the process of development.

In the second place, 'development' is far too broad a notion to use as underpinning for political action. Given the generally positive overtones of the concept, many strategies and projects can be legitimised by the claim that they will produce development. Opposition to programmes can be neutralised by recourse to the presumed general wealth-enhancing effects that they have, since narrow group interests arguably should not stand in the way of achieving a 'greater good for a greater number of people'. In this vein, even those projects that involve coercive forms of dispossession can be to an extent legitimised by the claim that they will lead to development.

Building on the criticism brought forward in this part of the book, the next chapters contain a discussion of what is, we feel, a better understanding of development and the role of politics in this process. Structural political economy, based on an understanding of development as conflict, and of politics as struggle, offers an alternative for the assertion that development results from the elimination of collective action problems and the creation of institutions that are able to serve an unproblematic 'common interest'. We turn to a discussion of structural political economy in the awareness that ignoring the reality of conflict 'only leads to bewilderment in the face of its manifestation and to impotence in dealing with [it]' (Mouffe, 1993: 140).

Part II
Applying Structural Political Economy

5
Understanding the Development Problem

Introduction

In previous chapters we have critiqued the ways in which donors and associated researchers have attempted to incorporate political economy analyses into their approaches to development. In particular, we identified three assumptions which are prevalent among aid practitioners but which constrain the effectiveness of their political economy approaches: namely, the assumption that development is a public or common good; the assumption that correct development policies can be identified and implemented through experts and enlightened reformers working in partnership; and the assumption that failure by political elites to identify and implement such policies emerges from either information failures or perverse incentives, that is collective action problems. In this second part of the book, we offer a counter proposal to each of these assumptions, developed on the basis of structuralist political economy, and illustrated through reference to four case studies of aid projects in Southeast Asia. In this chapter, we elaborate on our understanding of development as a process of contested structural change, and the implications of this for aid programming.

Development is often equated with the projects and programmes of donors and governments and the positive outcomes to which these aspire. The outcomes can be measured in different ways: through narrow monetary indicators such as growth in Gross Domestic Product; or through broader measures evaluating levels of health, literacy and life expectancy, alongside measures of income, as in the United Nations

Development Programme (UNDP)'s human development model. Positive outcomes in these terms, and therefore development itself, are regarded as a public good, objectively known and uncontested by the broader population once benefits are felt, provided such populations are rational and properly informed. However, within a framework of structuralist political economy, donor activities around policy-making and project design are better referred to as *aid programming*, since they represent an intervention in larger, transformational processes. We argue taking the politics of aid programming seriously requires recognition that development is a historical process of contested structural change. Aid programming is an intervention in this process, but is not a driver of it.

Development as contested structural change

Development as contested structural change comprises the emergence of new social orders which are based on fresh ways to create wealth and sustain power. The significance of social orders for aid programming is that they are relatively enduring and not purposefully changed without a shift in power relations and/or perceptions of interests. A structuralist approach is one which pays due attention to this historical context of development, a context which combines both opportunities for and constraints on the activities of individuals and groups. Hence, structures are not determinants of agency; they are rather the historically produced features of a given social order which require empirical analysis in their own right to establish their connection to actual agency (see Hay, 2002).

The nature of the economy is a key structure since it throws up different class-based social forces, with different capabilities to change their relative position vis-à-vis other groups. The nature and power of these groups are controlled significantly by their position within the economic order – as landlords, subsistence farmers, shareholders, factory workers, informal hawkers and so on. However, within these constraints, which of the possible trajectories of development are in fact realised depends upon contingent political strategies – the investments, expropriations, protests, strikes, alliances, negotiations, subversions and evasions – in which the various actors engage. On this basis, what matters for development outcomes are the kinds of social forces involved, their interests and how they are organised in relation to different social agendas (Robison, 2012: 10).

Viewed in this light, development is never merely a public good, but is rather a perpetual process of resource redistribution that is fought over by class-based groups. The emergence of new socio-economic orders on the back of, for example, privatisation of landholdings, emergence of plantation agriculture or technological innovations leading to industrialisation, is dependent upon the expropriation of particular types of resources by particular social groups. This expropriation is politically contested and requires elites to continually seek new and better means of consolidating power, in the face of perpetual efforts by dispossessed groups to prevent this. The process of expropriation of resources and consolidation of power is the essence both of politics and of development.

Donor projects are therefore interventions in ongoing political struggles over the trajectory and nature of the emerging social order. Because the outcome of economic restructuring for the poor is not predetermined, but the outcome of political struggle, scope may exist for donor interventions to assist the poor in winning material gains in their conditions of life. However, taking advantage of such opportunities requires a full appreciation of the political nature of such interventions, and their impacts in these terms.

Development as politics

The political struggles that constitute and drive the development process can be understood as operating on both material and ideological levels. The material level of struggle constitutes perpetual contention over allocations of resources emerging from the evolving productive process (Fine, 2006). Such struggles include contestation over privatisation of previously commonly or customarily held resources; over wages, rents, and the price of subsistence goods; and over taxation and relief policies. In many parts of the developing world, this is a struggle which is manifest in physical violence, exercised by police with batons evicting squatters from slums; by security guards beating up picketing workers; and by the violence and plunder perpetrated by marauding or invading armies.

However, structural accounts of power also emphasise more indirect forms of power: the ways in which power shifts political contestation into struggles over ideas conducted through non-violent processes such as debate, education, litigation, non-violent protest and even advertising campaigns. Ideological struggles invoke ideas about rights, custom, obligation, authority and expertise over such issues as the right to occupy particular spaces; to claim certain sorts of recognition or assistance; and to engage without interference in particular sorts of activities (see, for example, Hickey, 2012). These struggles are ongoing, even where physical resistance is less obvious, in contending narratives of progress, modernisation and development itself.

Institutions are important mechanisms for translating violent struggle into contestation on the ideological level. The emergence of political regimes which can transform violent confrontation into political debate has long been regarded as central to the 'liberal peace' promoted by international donor agencies in fragile or post-conflict states (Paris, 2004). By contrast, in our structural approach, institutions are contingent features of the social and political order that reflect the power relations inherent in that order and operate to promote their long-term stability and hence the long-term ascendancy of dominant forces within them (Poulantzas, 1978; Jessop, 2002; Sangmpam, 2007). The 'political settlements' literature makes this point but then underestimates the difficulty of intervening to make such settlements more inclusive (Di John and Putzel, 2009; Parks and Cole, 2010). Further, from a structural perspective, settlements can never be regarded as actually settled or sorted.

In an unequal society, institutionalisation, while often reducing the level of violence, does not therefore increase opportunities for the poor and consequently habituating the poor to an institutional order that does not serve them particularly well is likely to be difficult. Nevertheless, a disjuncture between the way institutions operate and the immediate interests of rulers can offer opportunities for subordinate groups to gain tactical advantage. For example, when rights are enshrined in law through political mobilisation, such laws may then become an avenue for subsequent demand-making, as when poor groups take out and win public interest litigation cases in the Indian court system (Goetz and Jenkins, 2005). If the poor can overcome problems of access to institutions, for example through gaining the support of advocacy NGOs, they can use such strategies to achieve short-term gains over particular concrete issues. But, because powerful groups have greater influence over the reform of institutions than weaker groups, in the long term the routing of struggle through institutions of governance perpetuates rather than ameliorates the dominance of the elite. Donor interventions which rely on the creation of institutions intended to redistribute power decisively away from a powerful elite are, therefore, in this model, unlikely to work very successfully (Hughes, 2009). Without concomitant shifts in power relations or elite political strategies, the implementation and enforcement of pro-poor institutions are likely to be resisted by the power-holders, hence undermining their performance and sustainability (Khan, 2010: 31–32).

Conceptualising development as politics, then, entails analysing contemporary developmental contexts as arenas of constrained political contestation. This contestation takes place between social groups whose political agency and creativity are powerfully restricted by historical processes and legacies that affect the size and cohesion of the group, their vital interests and level of organisation, and their ideas about themselves, about development and about politics, and their capabilities in defending all of these. Contestation takes place on a landscape that includes more or less powerful institutions, which significantly affect the kinds of political strategies that might be either possible or successful. However, these institutions are themselves relatively fluid and success in using a particular institution to further the cause of the poor today does not necessarily imply that similar success will be possible tomorrow.

Development as ideology

A political conception of development dispenses with the idea that there is a broadly unitary goal upon which developing economies are converging. Regarding development as the contingent outcome of political struggle between contending social forces implies that a range of different outcomes are desired and possible. Preference for one over the other is then partly a normative question, requiring answers that are based upon values – justice, efficiency, equality, etc. – rather than upon assertions of technical correctness. Exposing the normative basis of particular conceptions of development allows us to see discourses of development as ideological – as emanating from normative positions espoused by different groups attempting to advance their own interests. In this account, the term ideology denotes 'any systematic set of practical or theoretical ideas which articulate the interests of a group' (Gamble, 1981: 157).

The claim that development is a public good – something that will benefit everyone in the end – is itself an ideological claim, and particular strategies or projects, including those that involve coercive forms of dispossession, can be to an extent legitimised by the claim that they will lead to 'development'. Aid programming entails ideologies of development that of course are part of the political mix. Development agencies may privilege their approaches to development through claims of expertise and best practice, but they reflect alliances of power within and between donor countries. Identifying donor approaches as ideological does not imply an inability to distinguish between better or worse outcomes; it simply reminds us that the achievement or non-achievement of aspirations such as spreading literacy or lowering poverty is the result, not of right programming, but of contextually specific struggles over power.

In summary, understanding the varied record of success and failure of donor agency programmes in developing countries requires better analysis of the specific historical context and ongoing political struggles within which particular aid programmes have been rolled out. Such an analysis requires investigation of three empirical questions: *What are the social groups that are already engaged in struggle in the specific context relevant to the aid programme in which we are interested? How do these groups understand 'development' and how do they understand particular relevant development issues?* and *What political strategies do they have at their disposal to advance their position at the expense of others?* Answering these three questions offers a basis for assessing how, and how significantly, the proposals of the aid programme change the situation and for explaining, therefore, how different groups react to the programme.

Southeast Asian case studies

Four case studies of responses to governance reform programmes illustrate the utility of this type of analysis. The case studies used here, and in the next two chapters, are drawn from three countries in Southeast Asia, namely Cambodia, Indonesia and the Philippines. Two of the cases – that of a World Bank Demand for Good Governance programme in Cambodia and a participatory budgeting programme in Mataram in Indonesia – focus on the promotion of public participation as an antidote to corruption. The other two – an Asian

Development Bank (ADB) programme to provide social housing[1] for the poor in Metro Manila, and approaches to the governance of urban informal sector workers in Jakarta – focus on the programmes (or lack of programmes) to assist the urban poor. In each case, we demonstrate how local power-holders, activists and groups of the poor responded to new programmes and policies as tactical opportunities to achieve some kind of leverage in ongoing struggles over the distribution of resources – in these cases state budgets and urban land – and we show how these struggles are pursued through ideological contestation, political activism and, often, physical violence.

In two of these cases – one in Cambodia and one in Indonesia – good governance reform programmes were successful to the extent that something was actually implemented, even though, as the analysis will show, it is not clear that they achieved concrete improvements in governance. In both cases, good governance reform was designed to expand participation of the public and non-governmental organisations (NGOs) in decisions about the spending of money. Consequently, in each case issues to do with the role of corruption in the political economy of power were significant in determining the outcomes. In the other two cases, the issue at stake was how to allocate land in two capital cities, Metro Manila and Jakarta. In Metro Manila, the ADB's Urban Services for the Poor programme failed to get off the ground when the Bank was not able to reach agreement with envisaged local government implementers over the nature of the programme and its multi-million dollar loan was withdrawn (ADB, 2010). In Jakarta, the issue of the informal economy's contribution to the city's future development is one which neither government nor international donor agencies have chosen to address or invest in. In each case, explaining what happened requires combining an understanding of the structural context with an analysis of the political strategies employed by key actors.

In this chapter, the development problem is introduced in each case, and the nature of the actors involved is set out. In the next chapter, we explain the political strategies of the various reform actors, and how these might support or impede the aid programmes in question. Then, in Chapter 7 we consider what this means for understandings of the relationships between donors and other political actors in specific aid contexts and, therefore, what it means to provide aid for development.

Contexts for good governance: Cambodia

A low income, post-conflict country, Cambodia nevertheless achieved spectacular rates of economic growth in the ten years from 1998 to 2008, averaging almost 10 per cent GDP growth per year. Between 1993 and 2007, the percentage of the population living in poverty (defined as per capita income of less than US$0.61 per day) declined from 47 to 30 per cent and is thought to have declined further since, prompting suggestions that Cambodia may have achieved its Millennium Development Goal of halving poverty by 2015 in 2009 (World Bank, 2013a). However, over the same period inequality has widened dramatically, within urban areas, between urban and rural areas, and within rural society. 12 per cent of households are 'food insecure' and Cambodia remains one of 30 countries worldwide where levels of hunger and malnutrition are classified as 'alarming' (UNDP, 2012). The World Bank sums up the views of many of Cambodia's international donor agencies when it comments on its website that the pursuit of good governance continues to be a challenge (World Bank, 2013a).

The facts contained in the above paragraph represent the conventional summary of Cambodia's recent past and current status as a beneficiary of international aid, drawn from two fairly standard country 'overviews' from the UNDP and the World Bank. However, they give almost no sense of where power lies in Cambodia, how politics has interacted with processes of economic production and consumption to give rise to the distribution of resources hinted at above, and what kinds of societal actors have benefited or, conversely, been marginalised by the events of the past two decades. It is clear from the World Bank's rather acerbic remark that Cambodia has not responded to World Bank advice by promptly and/or successfully implementing the type of reforms the World Bank prescribes. However, no explanation is offered as to why not, or how, in that case, governance does function in Cambodia, and how aid agencies might alter their policies in Cambodia as a consequence.

Understanding governance in Cambodia requires an analysis of the kinds of social forces that have emerged in Cambodia in the context of post-colonial state building, Cold War violence and post-Cold War reconstruction. These social forces constitute the drivers who, with various means at their disposal, determine responses to reform, and understanding their nature, interests and power base is necessary to explain their reactions (Hughes, 2009).

The key social forces that exist in Cambodia today principally eme-rged from the wreckage of the collapse of the Khmer Rouge regime in the late 1970s. In the 1980s the regime formally espoused Vietnamese-style socialism; however, in the aftermath of the disastrous Khmer Rouge experiment with collectivisation, the credibility of any kind of socialist ideology was fairly low in the Cambodian countryside, and consequently the government refrained from pushing ideologi-cal agendas too forcefully, focusing instead upon the pressing needs of raising recruits for the army and acquiring sufficient rice from the rural population to feed the cities. By the time free market reforms were enacted by the end of the 1980s, there already existed in Cambodia a landed peasant class and a small business elite, largely comprised of former state officials.

The free market reforms benefited state officials who were in a position to pocket the proceeds. There was uncontrolled and under-regulated privatisation, not only of agricultural land but also of state-owned enterprises, state land and forests, and government buildings. Initially land ownership rights were awarded to those already farm-ing the land; however, the violent and predatory nature of the state, and the inaccessibility, incompetence and corruption of the judiciary paved the way for rapid concentrations of landholdings in the hands of the wealthy and well-connected. Cambodia has shifted from hav-ing a remarkably equal distribution of wealth in 1989 when land rights were formally granted to the tillers, to a highly unequal distri-bution, particularly in rural areas, and particularly in areas of rapid natural resource exploitation (STAR Kampuchea Organisation, 2007; World Bank, 2007a).

Hence, in the course of the 15 years since the United Nations elections in Cambodia, a rapid and drastic social stratification has occurred. This has happened alongside a consolidation of control by the ruling Cambodian People's Party (CPP). The ability of the CPP to mobilise high levels of electoral support in this unpromising context is due to the way that the Party has used political development funds to ameliorate the potentially destabilising effects of rising landless-ness and worsening inequality. During the course of the 1990s, the CPP pursued a strategy of consolidating loyalty among key sections of the elite, specifically key individuals in the police and military, among defecting insurgent units, and in subnational administration. This was achieved through offering these individuals the opportunity to amass fortunes through participation in a programme of asset stripping, primarily with respect to Cambodia's forests and fisheries, mostly located in remote and insecure areas.

Cambodian businessmen with links to the CPP have benefited from lucrative contracts in a range of sectors from forestry to plantation agriculture, to import-export, electricity supply, banking and tourism, in return for contributing to the activities of the Party. Using a reconstructed version of traditional patron–client relations, the Party has embedded itself firmly within the state apparatus, local government and, increasingly, civil society operations by fostering personalised networks of loyalty cemented through the provision of financial contributions, gifts, and public works projects.

It is important to note that, for the Party, this constitutes development, a claim that is evidenced, from their perspective, by Cambodia's remarkable rate of economic growth and its moderate success in reducing poverty. This approach to development is predicated upon a number of key ideological assumptions held by Party leaders that have changed little over the past 30 years: that the key problem is order and stability, and only the CPP is sufficiently powerful to prevent a slide back into warfare and/or chaos; that consequently the key goal of governance is to distribute resources in a manner that will promote loyalty to the Party; and that therefore governance arrangements should function in a manner which maximises the discretionary power available to key power-holders.

These ideological assumptions contrast sharply with those held by Cambodia's donors, who have continually but unsuccessfully pressed for reforms that would better separate party and state, reduce the state's demands on business for informal contributions, and regularise state–business relations as a means to stimulate competition. Significantly, however, donors do not entirely reject the CPP's concerns about stability. There has been some lack of zeal, on the part of bilateral donors in particular, for pressing for governance reforms in Cambodia precisely because the CPP is regarded as reliable in terms of maintaining control of a population that has been historically unruly.

The success with which this project has been pursued by the Cambodian government is facilitated by two key factors. The first is the regional investment climate, particularly in the decade from 1999 to 2009, and the regional demand for commodities such as timber and cash crops which Cambodia was able to supply. This produced a willing stream of investors prepared to cooperate with the CPP development projects, in return for access to land, timber and other resources. The second important factor is the political strategies pursued to severely weaken any organised opposition. Cambodia has a long history of suppression of civil society going back to colonial times. This has continued, albeit less heavy-handedly, to the present. This means that opposition to the CPP's project has largely been sporadic and disorganised, despite the fact that the United Nations peacekeeping mission brought a new constitution that enshrined liberal political and civil rights.

Reliance on the private sector to provide the resources for this form of governance has produced a regime characterised by massive corruption and a laissez-faire attitude towards expropriation and stripping of assets by state officials and their private sector partners. Enclosure of common resources has prompted a significant degree of conflict, as poor Cambodians have struggled to retain access to informally settled land, forests, fisheries and water resources. Often, this conflict has taken the form of violence in the context of forced evictions, strikes and, to some extent, public protests. The Cambodian Government has generally avoided prosecuting officials or business people responsible for abusive acts in these contexts, even when blatant human rights abuses have occurred.

Understanding the political economy of the CPP's re-emergence over the past ten years is essential to understanding the success or failure of various good governance reform programmes. The Party is reliant for its control on the ability to enforce networks of loyalty through the generation of slush funds to provide rewards and through the ability to make credible threats of punishment for disloyalty. Therefore it needs to ensure that governance works to promote the interests of loyalists and exclude dissidents. This has led to continued politicisation of the judicial system, refusal to act meaningfully to tackle corruption, and the use of the military and police to advance the private interests of property owners over the interests of the poor.

The Cambodian government accepted the World Bank's proposal for a Demand for Good Governance programme in Cambodia – a proposal that entailed training civil society groups in social accountability techniques such as parallel budgeting or participatory planning, as a means to better provide oversight of Cambodian government activities, particularly at local levels. Interestingly, while the Cambodian government was prepared to adopt the scheme, the name was changed, on translation into Khmer to the 'Local Governance Programme' because the government 'does not accept that anyone has the right to demand good governance from us'.[2] Furthermore, the government reserved the right to channel the project money to NGOs already considered sympathetic to the government: 'We are very clear: anyone who opposes the government will not be funded'.[3] Finally, participants in the programme commented that the context in Cambodia – a context characterised by a deteriorating human rights situation and a narrowing of public space – was not similar to the environment in India and the Philippines where social accountability techniques were initially developed. The technical ability to create a parallel budget does not necessarily translate into the political ability to confront the government with evidence of corruption, in a state where a recent anti-corruption law stipulates that whistle-blowers making accusations that do not lead to convictions face a heavy fine or potentially a jail sentence (RGC, 2010). As a result of these contextual factors, the Demand for Good Governance programme, although generating a gaggle of fairly marginal projects, has not produced much momentum for change.

Contexts for participatory governance: Indonesia

Contemporary governance in Indonesia must be understood against the backdrop of 15 years of post-authoritarian transformation, preceded by three decades of Cold War authoritarianism. The shattering consequences of the Asian Financial Crisis of 1997–1998 for both the economy and the regime produced major governance transformations, including democratisation, the retreat of the military from politics, the expansion of civil liberties and civil society, and a radical programme of decentralisation (Aspinall and Fealy, 2003). These developments reflect a reorganisation of power, but, it has been argued, not a fundamental transformation (Robison and Hadiz, 2004; Hadiz, 2010).

Although the Asian Financial Crisis was profoundly destabilising, the reconfiguring of Indonesian governance in its aftermath occurred within constraints set by the nature of the economy and the legacies of the past. The economy, somewhat like that in Cambodia, has been described as an unconstrained form of robber baron capitalism (Robison, 2006: 111). The privatisation of state monopolies in the 1970s and 1980s created coalitions of private and public oligarchies that acted politically to secure their own interests. Political strategies

employed ranged from the massacres of communists and trade union-
ists in the 1960s, through the creation of a military command
reaching down to village level, to bureaucratic control of the press,
emasculation of the political opposition and tight regulation of civil
society. As in Cambodia, the 'disorganisation' of civil society and close
relations between the state and indigenous business entailed the flour-
ishing of corruption and the consolidation of wealth and power in the
hands of unaccountable elites.

Following the Asian Crisis, Indonesia has developed genuine but
weak forms of democratic politics, such as a free press and an elected
parliament, that live in uneasy political accommodation with a corrupt state–business elite. Both electoralism and decentralisation of
governance have prompted a diffusion of power among a wider set
of elites at local as well as national levels. However, 'money politics'
remains central to the way in which these elites contend, ensuring that
predatory political and economic interests remain closely tied to one
another. The weakness of civil society – a legacy of the Soeharto era –
entails there are few mass movements that are capable of influencing
or constraining, on a day-to-day basis, the activities of politicians. A
variety of NGOs exist; many of them capable of interacting with government and staging protest movements on occasion. However, since
the consolidation of the post-Soeharto era, and particularly under the
presidency of Susilo Bambang Yudhoyono from 2004 to 2014, such
movements tend to be localised and, although sometimes capable of
gaining concessions from state actors, have rarely threatened business
as usual within government.

Our case study of good governance reform in Mataram, the provincial capital of West Nusa Tenggara Province, located on the island
of Lombok, focused on an aspect of Indonesia's decentralisation
reforms, enacted in early 2001. The decentralisation programme
was intended to decisively undermine remnant networks persisting
from the Soeharto era, including through the institution of local
participatory planning processes, known as *Musyawarah Perencanaan
Pembangunan* or *Musrenbang*. The extent to which this goal has been
achieved, however, is disputed, and *Musrenbang* have emerged as sites
for struggle between coalitions of reformers, local elites and more
centralised actors (Wilson et al., 2009).

Decentralisation was enacted decisively in Indonesia following the
end of the New Order era but, importantly, did not arise from the

demands of civil society or the poor. Rather it occurred because local leaders, particularly in resource-rich regions such as Aceh, Riau, East Kalimantan and Papua, grasped the opportunity presented by the end of authoritarian rule to secure a greater share of national wealth through claiming greater regional say over political and economic policy (Aspinall and Fealy, 2003: 2). As ethnic violence flared in a number of regions following the fall of the regime, local politicians used populist appeals to local identity to empower these demands (ibid., 3). However, Hadiz (2003: 123) contends that, 'though often expressed in terms of local pride, or ethnic or regional identity versus national unity', the contest has been mainly over control over resources. With the erosion of central authority in the context of the Asian Financial Crisis, the *reformasi* uprising and Soeharto's resignation, the state was forced to accommodate these demands (Hadiz, 2003: 122). Local elites then swiftly took advantage of decentralisation to raise taxes and purse development projects.

In Mataram, civil society organisations have made great efforts to promote citizen's engagement in the local participatory planning and budgeting processes arising from decentralisation. However, how these civil society organisations have emerged is important and needs to be understood against the backdrop of the city's changing political economy. Social structure on Lombok Island in the past reflected the island's agricultural base, with a clear divide between a traditional elite and the mass of peasant farmers and agricultural labourers (Kristiansen et al., 2004). However, the increase in political and economic importance of provincial capitals under decentralisation has coincided with a tourist boom on Lombok, giving rise to ten years of inward migration, urbanisation and economic growth. This has produced a more multicultural society and a new middle class, significantly altering, although not entirely overturning, the local balance of power.

The new middle class has been an important source of Mataram's current crop of civic associations. These vary from religious-based organisations through advocacy groups to health organisations. Some civil organisations were formed and supported by local authorities as a means to promote particular policies and regulations. However, others are relatively independent, claiming a watchdog role vis-à-vis government activities, and implementing advocacy programmes aimed at empowering people at the grass roots level (Kaffah and Amrulloh, 2003). They are often seen as a new force that can challenge government power, and as such have often been met with suspicion or repression by local authorities. Corruption is a specific concern for the city's varied civil society organisations, reflecting the significance of this issue in ideologies of development in the post-Soeharto era Indonesia more broadly.

Across the country there is a dedicated anti-corruption NGO movement (Setiyono and McLeod, 2010: 349), although it has a limited, organised constituency base. Many of the activists in these NGOs cut their teeth in the student-led *reformasi* movement, whose rallying cry was 'corruption, collusion, and nepotism' (*korupsi, kolusi, dan nepotisme* or *KKN*). For the *reformasi* activists, corruption was linked to the systemic abuse of power by Soeharto, his family and cronies; therefore, its widespread continuation is seen to threaten Indonesia's political progress towards democracy (Rodan and Hughes, 2014: 146). Democratic concerns about corruption are distinct, in ideological terms, from neoliberal ones, but alliances of democratic and neoliberal reformers have nevertheless occurred, especially in the wake of donor funding (Rodan and Hughes, 2014: 4–17). Religious organisations, whose links to the Indonesian masses are far deeper than those of NGOs, have also become involved in the anti-corruption debate, but have taken a moral rather than a specifically democratic approach. In this political environment, politicians have been pressured to adopt an anti-corruption agenda even while anti-corruption institutions are being undermined.

In Mataram, open access to participation in the process of local government budget preparation and implementation has become an increasingly important demand of civil society – indeed the city is regarded as something of a showcase for this kind of activism. NGOs, journalists, academics and religious organisations have teamed up to conduct a range of activities in this area, with funding from international agencies such as The Asia Foundation and the Ford Foundation.

For the Mataram civil society activists, participation in budgeting and planning processes offers more than just a watchdog role. In strategic terms, they see it as providing an opportunity to contribute substantively to articulating critical conceptions of development that can benefit a much wider section of society. However, although activists recognise this potential, their ability to realise it is undermined by several constraints, which reflect two key features of the context. First, civil society organisations remain highly fragmented and compete for scarce resources. Second, corruption remains a key means by which governments reward supporters and maintain control, in a social and political order in which many existing power-holders retain a strong stake. Consequently, both within civil society and within government, powerful actors actively seek to undermine the anti-corruption movement, or at least to constrain anti-corruption activists within existing hierarchies of power.

As a part of their political strategies, civil society activists in Mataram have attempted to forge alliances with two other key groups with influence over the *Musrenbang* process – lawmakers and bureaucrats. Some elected members of the Mataram parliament are committed to reform and have been able to use their own function in legislation, budgeting and oversight to attempt to make the annual budgeting process more accessible and responsive. The relationship that has emerged is a symbiotic one, in which civil society activists assist lawmakers in analysing and critiquing budgets and budget processes, and offer informal training to lawmakers. At the same time, lawmakers have better access to state documents than civil society activists and can pass on information that has been denied to citizens because of an entrenched culture of secrecy within the state apparatus.

There are also a number of reform-minded bureaucrats who form part of the coalition that attempts to promote more substantive participation through *Musrenbang* processes. Within the intermediate level of the local bureaucracy in Mataram is a group of 'young reformers', mainly located within the *Badan Perencana Pembangunan Daerah (BaPPEDA)* Kota Mataram, a vital unit in regional development planning. As with the NGO activists, many were previously members of student movement organisations during their undergraduate studies in various universities in Indonesia. These reformers have tried to promote a 'new corporate culture' in the local bureaucracy, and have actively built links with parliament members and civil society activists. This allows bureaucrats to supply important and urgent information to parliamentarians and civil society organisations.

Despite these promising initiatives, however, reformists in Mataram have had difficulty in actually using the *Musrenbang* process to achieve results. In part this is due to the weight of bureaucratic resistance to reform. Participatory budgeting and planning processes are routinely blocked by state officials seeking to insulate oligarchs from popular pressures. The *Musrenbang* remains an 'invited space' rather than a 'popular space'. Consequently, elites and local apparatchiks are over-represented, while people's participation is often cosmetic rather than substantive. Appointed officials are often invited to participate in place of elected officials, and local officers limit the duration of meetings to check popular participation. Information is provided only to official facilitators and not to ordinary citizen representatives. The process is couched in technical terms in order to limit the ability of ordinary people to comment substantively, despite NGO efforts to promote public awareness and education through 'Budget Schools'. Moreover, local officers have frequently already drawn up lists of priorities before the *Musrenbang* processes run. Thus one official commented: 'Policy making in the municipality of Mataram remains a top-down process. It is from the top to the bottom ... so citizens' proposals are useless'.[4]

These kinds of barriers to participation represent a hijacking of the planning process by the elite. In this context, cracks have appeared in the reformist coalition in Mataram. Civil society activists, in particular, distrust lawmakers and bureaucrats who have failed to help them when things get tough. In the words of one: 'We cannot expect too much from young bureaucrats. I see them being too pragmatic and curry-ing favour from superiors in order to keep their power network.'[5] The reformist bureaucrats, despite their best efforts, remain trapped within an institutional context that is oriented towards protection of oli-garchs and corrupt officials, rather than towards reform. As with social accountability initiatives in Cambodia, there is a disconnect between the democratising intent of *Musrenbang* institutions and the bureau-cratic dominance and political violence that overshadows them. This disconnect allows development planning to continue to be the sole province of private interests, oligarchs and corrupt officials.

Contexts for urban governance: Jakarta

Our two remaining case studies focus on urban governance in two of Southeast Asia's large and problem-ridden capital cities, Jakarta and Metro Manila. In both cases, the key question is how governance of development affects the poor. Interestingly, in each case, neoliberal ideological approaches to development, which regard the poor as active promoters of development through their own small-scale entre-preneurship, contrast sharply with the approaches of urban governors and mayors. In both cities, officials have prioritised capital-intensive development by big business, with the latter often owned or linked to powerful families who also dabble in politics. Development in these cities involves a daily struggle on the part of the poor to defend the marginal spaces in which they live and work from being consumed by mega-developments, or simply 'cleaned up'.

The Jakarta case study focuses on governance of the informal sector, a sector which includes a wide variety of income-generating activities, including casual jobs, small-scale entrepreneurial activity and home industries; that is, work existing generally outside of formal regulation and taxation by the state.[6] While informal sector workers are not necessarily poor, the poor are highly represented in the informal sector. The World Bank estimates that 60 per cent of all Indonesians, and 75 per cent of poor Indonesians, worked in the informal sector in the mid-2000s (World Bank, 2006: 37; also Khalik, 2008). Life in this sector is insecure, fluid and increasingly illegal as a result of government efforts to strictly contain it. Because ability to secure a livelihood is dependent upon ability to find space to occupy, informal sector workers frequently have to move and problems related to employment are often linked to problems relating to housing. These features of life in the informal sector make informal sector workers highly vulnerable to harassment or predation by state officials. This has increased since political decentralisation in 2001 gave provincial- and district-level governments a greater direct interest in urban development and revenues generated locally.

Street vendors are one of the more visible and contentious sections of the informal sector in Jakarta. Due to the often transient and fluctuating nature of street trading it is impossible to establish accurately the numbers involved, especially during periods of economic downturn and crisis when the numbers can swell significantly very quickly. Historically, street trading in urban public spaces has been relatively tolerated in Jakarta, provided it has not conflicted with other, more powerful interests. However, this tolerance lacked any legal foundation or formal safeguards. Instead, street vendors are informally governed on a daily basis, either by social dynamics within the poor communities themselves, or often additionally by criminal gangs, working collaboratively with the police, civil ordinance officials and local authorities (Robison et al., 2008). These gangs and officials commonly force informal sector workers to pay a variety of fees, in return for the chance to continue to operate in the city. But such informal arrangements are tenuous and can crumble quickly, without prior warning. Increasingly, there are regular violent confrontations between informal sector workers and government agencies as a result of amendments to 'public order' laws in 2008 making it illegal to sell goods or conduct business in streets and parks or other public places, expect in those areas designated for this purpose by the governor. Thus, the size and number of tolerated areas for street trading are shrinking inexorably.

In the post-authoritarian era, resources, space and infrastructure in Jakarta have been steadily appropriated in partisan ways by powerful interests. Most urban planning processes are carried out through negotiations between public and private sector actors (Hudalah and Woltjer, 2007). Consequently, land-use zoning and the attendant allocation of building permits are very susceptible to sweetheart deals, and are therefore highly biased against the interests of the informal sector (Wilson, 2006; Rukmana, 2007). There is also significant evidence that police, developers and so-called land mafia collude to illegally clear vendors and poor communities as a means to free up land for development (Human Rights Watch, 2006). Indeed, a 2009 report by the Indonesian human rights group *Imparsial* recommended that the *Satpol PP* (*Satuan Polisi Pamong Praja* or Civil Service Police Unit) be disbanded in view of its systematic human rights violations in the enforcement of public order laws against street vendors (*Imparsial*, 2009). *Satpol PP* raids are sporadic and usually involve no prior negotiation, thus increasing the likelihood of violent clashes. Often given no other place to go, evicted vendors simply relocate to another area, often to return to where they were once circumstances have eased. This contributes to the ongoing pattern of 'semi-nomadism' among informal sector workers.

Where there have been some legal protections for informal sector workers introduced – for example the regulations banning retail developments within 2.5 kilometres of traditional markets – the usual practice is for developers to buy themselves out of this requirement via illegal payments to public officials.[7] An outcome of this is an overabundance of high-end retail developments, housing estates and commercial buildings. For example, Jakarta has around 40 traditional markets, each of which can accommodate around 500 traders, or 20,000 in total.[8] This is well short of the estimated number of street vendors that the urban economy supports. By contrast, there are more than 60 medium to large shopping malls in Jakarta, estimated to be afforded by only around 500,000 residents, or just 3.5 per cent of the

city's population (Rukmana, 2009). The amount of land outside traditional markets designated for informal vendors has been continually
reduced to 'tidy up' the city (Sabarini, 2009). Meanwhile, the scale of
developments at the high-end is unsustainable as their contribution to
recurrent flooding and land subsidence is well established.

In the context of increasing competition and clashes of interests
over the use of public space in Jakarta, successive governors have
employed ideological representations of street vendors as criminal and
disruptive or – in the case of their city 'beautification' schemes – as
persistent 'eyesores'. One rationale for an intensification of repression
has been that large numbers of informal sector workers are economic
migrants to the nation's capital and that the capacity of the city to sus-
tainably absorb a greater population has already been surpassed. This
rationale is not entirely unfounded: Jakarta's population has grown
rapidly, from 1.5 million in 1950 to 9.58 million in 2010, with the
greater Jakarta region now being home to 26.6 million people, making
it one of the largest cities in Southeast Asia (*BPS*, 2010). In 2005 it was
estimated that Jakarta had 2.4 million long-term and 430,000 short-
term migrants from rural areas (Resosudarmo et al., 2009).

Contending portrayals of the informal sector in Jakarta illustrate
the irreconcilable conflicts of interests entailed in ideas about development. For the poor, for migrants from rural areas, and for low-paid
formal sector workers, the informal sector offers a vital source of both
income and affordable services. On the other hand, for the property
developers speculating on a future for Jakarta as a centre of luxury
hotels and up-market retail outlets, the mere presence of the informal
sector, not to mention the space it takes up, is considered a problem.
Despite some periodic recognition of the importance of the informal
sector as a social safety net, and a few associated attempts to accommodate the sector's needs, successive governors have responded much
more readily to big business interests and their overtures. Thus, in
addition to laws that criminalise the use of public space by street vendors, developers are not prosecuted for their violations of the few legal
provisions to protect informal sector activity.

Due to their marginal status, informal sector workers find it difficult
to develop political strategies to combat their increasingly criminal-
ised status. Many informal sector workers lack Jakarta identity cards
for one or more reasons: because they are not eligible for them, cannot
afford them, lack the documentation required to get one or simply

prefer not to interact with government officials. Without an identity card they are unable to vote in city elections and hence do not attract attention from political parties. Government offices that serve the informal sector tend to be largely powerless, as evidenced by the budgets of the Cooperatives and Small and Medium Enterprises Agency and worker health clinics. In 2009, while the *Satpol PP* were funded to the tune of 303 billion rupiah (US$31.2 million), the Cooperatives and Small and Medium Enterprises Agency received 64 billion rupiah (US$6.6 million) and the health clinics received 200 billion rupiah (US$20.6 million) (*Imparsial*, 2009).

Some sectoral civil society organisations, such as the Indonesian Street Traders Association, have emerged to engage in advocacy on the part of street vendors, and national labour unions, such as the Indonesian Prosperity Trade Union, have made some attempt to organise in the informal sector. However, these efforts remain limited and are problematic because of the sector's significant heterogeneity (Social Alert International, 2005). Otherwise, there are many local and national NGOs and community groups – such as the Jakarta Residents Forum (FAKTA) – involved in community organising and advocacy that have had some success in achieving local accommodations for the sector. Overall the informal sector workers' relative political weakness is a reflection of the nature of the sector itself and the powerful interests it confronts.

In summary, the context of informal sector work in Jakarta is a highly unequal one, in which poor, disenfranchised and marginalised people, despite their enormous numbers, have few political strategies to bring to bear against the combined forces of property developers, government officials and criminal gangs. The latter groups have employed exclusionary ideologies of development and significant capacities for violence in pursuit of material interests they share with political and economic elites. As a result, not only are there few formal or informal safeguards for street vendors, but their concerns have rarely made it onto any kind of reform agenda.

Contexts for housing governance: the Philippines

The final case study focuses on the ADB's Urban Services for the Poor programme to assist the Philippine government in a phased roll-out of a 15-year slum upgrading and eradication programme in Metro Manila. The programme aimed to help the Philippine government address the shelter needs of informal settler or urban poor households who make up about 43 per cent of the Metro Manila population (ADB, 2010). It sought to provide 'decent and affordable housing, basic infrastructure and urban services, including secure tenure' through a mix of investment financing, technical assistance, capacity building and local livelihood programmes (ADB, 2008b). Much of this approach is already officially Philippine government policy, with local governments responsible for ensuring that land, essential services and infrastructure are provided for social housing. However, compliance has typically been weak. One view is that this is because local governments frequently do not have suitable land. The ADB's plan was to assist with the 'integrated urban development' of lands being released for private sale by the national government, of which local governments would secure a 40 per cent share. By shifting the informal settlers on-site from the high to lower value areas, the authorities would 'realize higher commercial returns from the land without having to evict illegal tenants' who in turn would secure tenure and 'continue living close to their established livelihoods' (ADB, 2005: 8).

The programme was the product of, on the one hand, current international thinking on slum upgrading as a means to reduce urban poverty and, on the other hand, the policy and institutional frameworks for socialised housing in the Philippines. Importantly, both these stipulate alternatives to the failed strategies of forced eviction and relocation. In international policy circles, this is a legacy of research and advocacy which has promoted more positive interpretations of slums as 'places of opportunity', not despair, where the poor can and should be encouraged to pursue their own 'self-help' strategies via market inclusion (UN-Habitat, 2003: xxvi).

However, the existing legal and institutional framework for socialised housing in the Philippines is less the product of expert opinion than it is an outcome of domestic political processes in the post-Marcos era especially. Slums in the Philippines emerged as a result of the decline of agriculture, failures to implement land reform and the eclipse of manufacturing by service industries as the major contributor to GDP. Following the stagnation of growth in manufacturing, lack of opportunities in rural areas prompted continued rapid urbanisation but new urban dwellers moved into low-waged service industries that never achieved significant unionisation, which resulted in a high and stable level of urban poverty.

In the 1970s and 1980s, even under authoritarian rule, the urban poor were involved in protests to defend their claim to secure tenure in the huge shanty towns that they had built in Metro Manila. Local defiance could be linked to formal organisations in the form of NGOs with domestic and international church connections and support. The core groupings in this pursued forms of community organising, intended to prepare local communities for 'confrontations with the powerful' (Carroll, 1998: 118). During the 1980s, Metro Manila urban poor communities were also exposed to the political networks and alliances of leftists in the struggle against the Marcos dictatorship. Following the fall of Marcos in 1986, the leftist movement fractured and declined. Some groupings remained active in urban poor communities, but generally in line with political mobilization efforts, rather than to find solutions to the immediate problems of the poor.

After the restoration of democracy in 1986, the national political space for urban poor demands was increased, particularly for the community organisers with church support. As a result, during the Aquino period, there were some significant institutional and legislative gains from lobbying, most notably the setting-up of the Community Mortgage Programme and the Presidential Commission on the Urban Poor and the passing of the 1992 Urban Development and Housing Act (UDHA) (RA 7279) (Karaos et al., 1995). Hot on the heels of the 1991 Local Government Code enacting political decentralisation, the UDHA law meant that 'local governments are ordered to meet legal requirements before a demolition, conduct a land inventory and beneficiary registration, and identify sites for socialized housing' (Karaos, 1997: 69). Under the Act, socialised housing is for 'the underprivileged and homeless', however, it is in fact directed specifically at the fate of existing informal settlements – thus indicating the extent to which the legislation 'is advocacy driven'.[9] Importantly, this also signals the extent to which the informal settler problem is related to particular land-use conflicts. Urban poor advocacy has some reach into the national political arena in Metro Manila; however, it remains very site-specific, whilst political decentralisation and the rapid pace of urban development have meant the impact of urban poor advocacy has declined.

Part of the problem is that the urban poor now mostly lack the 'coalitions strong enough to confront the mayors'.[10] There has been a decline in the number of middle-class activists prepared to join as community

organisers, but as well, urban poor organisations lack the 'institutionalised channels of access to representation in the power structures of
society' (Racelis, 2005: 87). NGOs have tended to retain connections
within the Catholic Church, and used them to obtain national-level
political access, but these are normally ad hoc and dependent on individuals. To some extent there have been positions secured on local and
national government boards and committees, but these have offered
limited representation and have not been a means to alliance building
(Hutchison, 2007). Where results have been achieved at local government levels, this has been an outcome of political pressures applied to
elected officials by local communities and NGOs.

In this period, urban poor advocates have generally considered the
ADB to be an ally, on account of its involuntary resettlement policies and its efforts in relation to particular projects and officials.[11] Yet
they stress they have received no direct support from the Bank. More
generally, during the 1990s, urban poor NGOs were given greater
'participatory' roles in mobilising communities for project and programme implementation, but these have been within the confines
of donors' hopes for social capital as a tool of development (Shatkin,
2007: 6–7). The ADB's belief in the poor as agents of development,
liberating themselves from poverty through entrepreneurship, at
least supports a policy position that is sympathetic to the desire of
the poor to remain in the city. It does not go so far as to tackle the
structural impediments that limit the ability of the poor to trade
their way out of poverty.

From the perspective of the national and local governments, investments in programmes for the poor are inherently unattractive. Mayors
tended to view their spending on socialised housing narrowly, as a
matter of investment and returns, rather than as part of a strategy to
assure better human development outcomes for the poor in the city.
This betrays the underlying vision of development animating local
government planning in Metro Manila. For many local governments,
slums are viewed less as evidence of market and governance failures, as
a problem in themselves – as 'urban blight' to be removed by development. Thus they preferred physical destruction and relocation of the
inhabitants to long-term strategies of support for the poor to invest
in and upgrade their own neighbourhoods. These attitudes reflect a
broader set of middle- and upper-class ideologies about the urban poor
and their settlements being an offence to *urbanidad*, a Tagalog word

denoting good manners or civility. Such views encourage a belief in development as improvement centred on the nexus between personal discipline and social order, cleanliness and morality and the beautification of the urban environment.

Under the 1991 Local Government Code – that mandated political decentralisation in the Philippines (a decade before Indonesia) – local governments were given primary responsibility for urban development and service delivery. Also, they were given greater revenue-raising powers through 'property taxes, proceeds from the operation of public enterprises (such as public markets), local business taxes' and so on (Capuno, 2002: 234). In Metro Manila, the local government revenues from such sources are well in excess of that which allotted by the national government (Shatkin, 2007: 36). In short, local governments largely consider that 'land is too precious a commodity to use for socialized housing, [for] a group that in their view is an impediment to the kind of urban development that is attractive to global capital' (Shatkin, 2007: 26). As outlined in the next chapter, the ADB programme required that a portion of land be set aside for social housing and this was a key reason why the mayors declined to sign on.

Conclusion

The introductions to the case studies above illustrate three key contentions about the relationship between aid and development. First, they show that aid programmes are interventions in ongoing struggles over resources in which combatants are already lined up and doing battle. A policy 'problem' such as a shanty town, an unsanitary street market or a leaky budget reflects a historical victory on the part of some group in capturing a particular set of resources – a victory that is usually in the process of being contested in some way by those who have lost out. Thus the sporadic protests against resource appropriation for patronage in Cambodia; the increasing concern of the Mataram middle class over corruption; the efforts of the urban informal sector workers to secure space for commerce in Jakarta; and the fight of the poor for tenure security in Metro Manila are all manifestations of class-based conflicts, and the logic of this struggle determines how local players respond to aid programmes.

Second, the case studies illustrate how different ideologies of development are important for the ways in which these struggles are played out and, hence, for the outcomes of aid programming. Normative visions of development goals and the means to achieve these reflect different material interests that are also in themselves a vital part of political positioning. International ideologies of development may intersect partly with these normative positions, and may come to inform and frame them to some extent, but they are unlikely to entirely displace them. More commonly, the development goals of slum eradication and good governance, for example, are appropriated and reinterpreted by elites as a tactic to deflect criticism, garner support or generally make the most of opportunities.

Third, each of these cases indeed reflects the significance of the ongoing context of violence in development in Southeast Asia. From authoritarian Cambodia to post-authoritarian Philippines and Indonesia, violence is a regular part of day-to-day struggle, whether in the context of violent repression of activists; forced evictions of squatters; demanding of money with menaces by gangs and police; or simply a climate of fear that is nurtured by a selective campaign of political assassination (Boudreau, 2009). The background threat of violence renders development a dangerous process for those engaged in it, particularly the poor, and severely compromises the utility of programmes based upon the establishment of institutions with which the poor would need to engage assertively in order to make them work.

This represents a significantly different portrayal of development than mainstream accounts of institutional malfunction, market failure and even collective action dilemmas. What, then, are the implications of this portrayal for donors attempting to work more politically in development? This is the subject of the remaining chapters.

6
Analysing Reform and Reformers

Introduction

In aid programming, working more politically is often taken to mean finding and supporting developmental reformers as agents of change. But given that everyone can claim to be a reformer when they talk with donor agencies, there is an urgent need for a form of analysis that can evaluate the commitment of actors involved. The reconceptualisation of development offered in the last chapter offers a basis for this. As aid programming is an intervention in ongoing development struggles, it is possible to gather significant information on how relevant actors conceive of and pursue their interests by analysing their stances in these struggles. Our analysis proceeds from the assertion that development actors differ in their conceptualisation of, and commitment to, particular reform goals, but they do so in a manner that is consistent with their broader interests and the ways they have pursued these over time.

If development is not a public good it is no longer sufficient to conceive of reformers as do-gooders and can-doers. Current approaches tend to look for the rarest of reformers – the committed and the influential. However, it is hard to find dedicated reformers among the politically powerful. Existing modes of governance operate over time in the interests of the dominant classes and to the detriment of opportunities for subordinate classes to gain control. Consequently, interest in reform by powerful groups is likely to be limited under normal circumstances and often self-serving. Among subordinate groups, on the other hand, reformers may be plentiful – motivated by their material hardship and marginalisation. Their interests in substantive reform are not likely to be realised, yet they may be able to exploit opportunities to make concrete gains in specific areas on occasions.

Working politically thus requires an understanding of the interests of reformers that draws upon evidence of their key concerns, their support bases, the way they understand their own authority and power, or marginalisation, and the positions they have sought to defend in consequence over time. These interests need to be understood within, and as emerging from, a dynamic context of political struggle. Analysis of this kind can help to distinguish between genuine concerns, tactical interests and hedging when power-holders talk about reform. Given that power-holders are more likely to be opportunists than idealists, it is especially important to understand how tactical interests emerge from relevant actors' broader political strategies. This then informs assessments of how far power-holders are likely to go along with a particular reform project, and at what point, or in what circumstances, are they likely to defect from it. The typology of reform actors presented in this chapter starts by distinguishing between those whose interests are aligned with the status quo and those who are not. First, however, we address how reform takes place.

Reform

Taking a structuralist approach does not imply that modes of governance are fixed and reform is not possible. Within this approach, reforms in governance practice are understood as arising in three ways. First, structures themselves are constantly changing, as capitalist development unfolds. Over the past 30 years, many countries in Southeast Asia have undergone drastic transformations through wars, trade and financial crises, closer regional and global economic integration, geopolitical shifts, and technological change. Yet, there are important continuities also. Powerful groups often continue to use tried and tested means to handle challenges, and even crises, until those means prove untenable. Thus, the second set of ways in which change takes place is through efforts by elites to experiment with modes of governance in order to refine the means by which their dominance is maintained.

Elite pacts that transition out of armed conflict or authoritarian rule, decisions to liberalise economies, amendments to electoral rules and laws on the governance of non-state organisations represent strategies by which elites attempt to refine the means by which they uphold their dominance. These changes occur as elites learn from one another and/ or respond to challenges from below. This implies that elite groups may initiate reforms either for reasons of pragmatism (to accommodate to a changing environment) or for opportunistic reasons (to cement an existing order rather than see it change). Our thesis, however, is that it is very rare for elites to initiate reforms because of conversion to a new set of ideals.

A third set of ways in which change takes place is through the strategic engagement of actors with institutions. As we have seen, structuralist political economy regards institutions primarily as sites of conflict between class-based alliances. The power of dominant groups entails that they erect institutions that are intended to bolster that power; however, subsequently, subordinate groups develop strategies for engaging with such institutions to contest elite control. Consequently, change can be prompted by judicial decisions, electoral mandates or administrative fiat. To the extent that these are prompted by mobilisation of subordinate social groups, such changes can produce positive outcomes from the poor, even if only limited.

Importantly, state institutions have a degree of autonomy from dominant groups in the social and political order that they uphold (Poulantzas, 1978). To this extent, the power of state officials to make concessions in response to challenges from below – concessions that are then binding on elites – operates in the interests of stabilising the political order over the long term.[1] Although state institutions can thus in some circumstances operate independently of elites and be quite responsive to demands from below, there are also limits to this. Over time, not only in fragile states but in any political system, institutions that fail to serve dominant forces will be reformed or sidelined. The way in which this is achieved will again depend on the political circumstances, including such factors as the extent of support for the relevant institution, the availability of ideologies that can be used to discredit the institution, and the degree of discomfort it is causing to the elite.

Structuralist political economy then offers an account of social and political change. However, except where a major crisis occurs that overturns the dominant class, political change tends to be promoted and enacted by powerful figures as a means to save the political order rather than to upset it. Hence, demands from below for far-reaching reform may be met by a variety of responses, ranging from conciliatory gestures or the sacrifice of an individual scapegoat to institutional changes that impose limits on elite power, to, in exceptional circumstances, genuine redistribution of greater power towards subordinate groups.

The impact of the Asian Financial Crisis on Indonesia's political institutions is an exemplar of this. The crisis was a major one, resulting in the resignation of the military dictator who had run Indonesia for the past 30 years. Soeharto's fall opened the way for democratisation, better respect for human rights, radical decentralisation and freedom of the press in Indonesia, all genuine reforms which have delivered real opportunities for activists seeking to promote greater social justice and democracy in Indonesia. However, significantly, few of Soeharto's business cronies or military enforcers were ever brought to trial for the gross abuses of power that occurred under Soeharto's rule. Nor has the new system fundamentally challenged Indonesia's economic, social and political order.

The case of Indonesia's post-New Order reform programme illustrates the contingency of even quite root-and-branch reforms to political regimes. These may be enacted when elites are under pressure, but then rolled back to an extent when the pressure eases off.

This account of political change has two implications. First, it means that donors, activists and others who seek to promote reform need to understand this differently. While 'Denmark' or some other approximation for good governance and/or social justice might be the ideal end point, the reality of reform is that it is an ongoing process of conflict, negotiation, compromise and accommodation. Understanding reform in this way entails paying more attention to concrete and achievable short-term outcomes that benefit groups suffering hardship, than to ideal end-states. This approach also suggests the inadvisability of compromising on important principles as a means to an end, since the end is highly uncertain and perpetually out of reach. Core values such as human rights and political openness need to be defended now or not at all. Working politically, for donor agencies and activists, means taking a clear stance on what is to be defended and the concrete outcomes worth pursuing for their own sake. The scope and ambition of achievable outcomes depend on political analysis of the level of support for reform and the likely sources of opposition. The second implication is that donors need to think about reformers differently.

Reformers

Identifying reformers does not mean finding individuals who combine high levels of influence with an unusual amount of gumption to reject the system that brought them to power in favour of a different, donor-promoted model. In normal times, such individuals are so exceptional as to be irrelevant to any kind of aid strategy. Rather, behind the rhetoric of 'partnership' and empty promises of compliance, donors are likely to encounter three categories of reformers (see Table 6.1). Distinguishing between these different types of reformer assists in analysing the politics of reform in terms of alliances. The first category of reformers is *idealists* who do want to fundamentally transform the system because it does not serve their material or ideological interests. However, except in times of deep crisis, these reformers are unlikely to be powerful. Where a situation is reasonably settled, those with power are those whom the system serves.[2] Indeed, idealist reformers are frequently unwilling to compromise with existing power-holders at all, since to do so could be to inadvertently legitimise the current system, and thus their ability to promote reform within the constraints of the existing social and political order is limited. When donors withdraw funding rather than compromise on programming goals, they are also idealists.

The second category of reformers is *opportunists*. These are individuals who are not interested in fundamental transformation of the system at all, but who manoeuvre to achieve a short-term tactical advantage. These individuals may be political leaders responding to

Table 6.1 Typology of reformers

Types of reformers	Types of alliances
Idealists: interested in reform in so far as it advances long-term goals of structural transformation	Form dedicated alliances only with ideologically like-minded actors; likely to reject tactical alliances
Pragmatists: have long-term goals of social transformation but also consider short-term gains significant	Form both dedicated alliances and tactical alliances
Opportunists: have short-term goals of self-interest; long-term goals unrelated to reform agenda. Hence commitment is contingent and tactical	Form tactical alliances

short-term problems – such as an upcoming election, an outbreak of unrest in a particular part of the country, or the need to negotiate with newly emerging social groups, such as a particular set of foreign investors or a newly formed trade union. Such leaders see particular donor programmes as offering opportunities to improve their bargaining position or to resolve a troublesome issue, and therefore cooperate tactically with the programme. The opportunist category may include both influential and non-influential individuals – indeed, some marginal players may use donor programmes tactically as an opportunity to access funds and/or achieve greater political influence. The key attribute of this group is that their interest in reform is self-serving, and therefore limited and contingent. Our contention is that reformism based upon ulterior motives can nevertheless be useful to both donors and activists for the poor, provided that both sides have a clear understanding of what the immediate goal of aid programming is and how the ulterior motives of powerful actors are likely to contribute to this.

Opportunists are unlikely to become converts to reform goals through participation in a programme. However, they may become more committed to a particular reform if they find that it promotes their power or the stability of the political order better than existing practices. They are also highly likely to bale if a programme outlives its utility. Thus, tactical alliances with opportunists are risky and unstable, in comparison with dedicated alliances with idealists, which more resemble the kinds of 'partnership' donors envisage. However, structural imperatives dictate that idealists, in normal times, are likely to comprise a marginal and uninfluential group. Except during times of political upheaval, the most powerful actors are likely to have gained their power by virtue of existing conditions, and therefore are unlikely to share long-term goals of social transformation. Tactical alliances with powerful opportunists offer a chance to implement measures which, even if limited or short-lived, can produce concrete improvements in the lives of the poor.

Between these two categories is a third which we call *pragmatists*. Pragmatists combine both a concern to fundamentally transform the system with the willingness to compromise in the short term to secure particular goals. This group may include power-holders who collaborate unwillingly with the system that brought them to power for fear of something worse. It may also include marginal players and their advocates seeking root-and-branch reform but willing to settle for some amelioration of hardship in the meantime. Pragmatists may be instrumental in driving ad hoc reforms, but may also lose interest if their willingness to compromise on long-term goals is pushed too far. Pragmatists have to balance obligations to their own more idealist constituencies on the one hand, with compromises that facilitate alliances with opportunists and idealists of a different ilk on the other. Understanding the political work that pragmatists do is important for donors, who are frequently themselves in the pragmatist camp.

Taking a political approach to understanding reformers implies a similar approach to understanding anti-reform interests. These are in turn likely to be a diverse set: some will regard their interests as directly challenged and hence will do their utmost to ruin the reform. These are *wreckers*. Others – in the category of *recalcitrants* – will not be directly challenged by the reform, but will regard participation in it as against their interests, perhaps out of loyalty to a group that is more directly opposed. These types of opponents can be distinguished from *obstructors* who do not necessarily oppose the reform itself, but may be engaged in activities or projects that inadvertently frustrate it. These different types are summarised in Table 6.2.

The final key group that it is necessary to identify is *gatekeepers*. These are groups that have a strategic importance to the progress of the reform because they control resources, expertise or access that is vital to the reform's success. Gatekeepers can be for or against reform, and may fall into any of the six categories identified in terms of their attitude to the reform, but their stance is particularly significant because they can make or break a reform agenda.

This analysis of reform actors draws attention to shifts in distributions of power among and within alliances, and the effect of this on

Table 6.2 Typology of non-reformers

Wreckers	Dedicated opponents: see their interests as directly threatened by the reform
Recalcitrants	Tactical opponents: their interests are not directly threatened by the reform, but they can see a tactical advantage in non-participation
Obstructors	Groups that are not necessarily opposed to the reform, but whose activities make the reform difficult (could include idealist reformers)

the ideological framing of reform agendas. Analysis of the relationships between class structure, power and ideology in the context of alliances of reform allows for richer appreciation of the way that strategies of contention are both constrained by context and continually evolving. It requires replacing broad visions of 'good governance' with ideas about concrete contributions that can be made to assist specific groups that donors desire to help. As such, this approach allows a more truly political analysis of the ways in which reform coalitions emerge and subside, of the support role that donors can play in that process and of the kinds of outcomes that are achievable given the power relations that prevail. Ultimately, the fate of particular programmes – as well as the path of reform overall – will reflect the way in which these actors engage in struggle in the dynamic setting of capitalist development and global integration.

Southeast Asian case studies

This is to be seen in our case studies, organised below as to the spectrum of their outcomes. In Metro Manila, material and ideological conflicts were a critical break on reform whereas in Cambodia, reform efforts failed once opportunism was exhausted. In Jakarta, the inherent disparities of power between street vendors and government led street vendors ultimately to refuse to engage at all in political negotiation as a part of a pragmatic strategy of self-preservation. In Mataram, idealist reformers were too weak politically to secure the potential gains from legislated reforms in the area of participatory budgeting.

Social housing in Metro Manila: a clash of ideals

The Asian Development Bank (ADB)'s Urban Services for the Poor initiative was a programme that foundered ultimately on the inability of all sides to find tactical or pragmatic common ground. As described in Chapter 5, the programme emerged from ideas about best practice in slum upgrading and poverty reduction within the ADB. The key was a proposal for 'land-sharing' – a form of mixed land use incorporating some high-value commercial developments and affordable social housing. The opportunity to rent or purchase affordable housing onsite is used to persuade informal settlers to vacate the part of the land that is slated for commercial development. Although local governments have to bear the cost of subsidising the housing, this is to be offset by new sources of revenue from the commercial development.

From the point of view of the ADB, this kind of approach provides a financially sustainable approach to urban development, while keeping the poor in the city as development actors. For the ADB, a key goal is not only to release land for high-value property developments, but also to integrate urban poor households into formal markets for land and money, as a means to enlist their entrepreneurial energies in the development project. Underpinned by the convictions of neoclassical economics, the ADB was convinced that the programme ought to make sound economic sense to Metro Manila local governments. However, the ADB's idealist stance on the need to forego some land for poor households was unacceptable to the mayors and they turned down the loan offers.[3]

Two of the local governments in the programme's first stage – those of Taguig and Quezon City – did have what they termed 'social housing' programmes in place, but they were not well suited to the needs of the urban poor. In Quezon City, socialised urban housing had been provided by a specially established Housing Urban Renewal Authority. However, this housing was directed at low-wage employees – particularly employees of city hall – whereas the poorest residents tended to have more precarious and informal income sources. A different city department, the Urban Poor Affairs Office, targeted the shelter needs of informal settlers, largely through a *national* government programme called the Community Mortgage Programme (CMP).[4] This programme provides low interest, subsidised financing for land acquisition, site development and home construction, although most of the funds are used for land acquisition (Porio et al., 2004). Consequently, the money is used predominantly to establish security of tenure rather than for slum upgrading. Although the scheme is popular, it has important limitations. The key criticism is that often the scheme does not produce any 'discernible change in [settlers'] way of living ... many CMP sites do not differ from other slum areas' (PBSP, 2007: iii). Furthermore, the CMP has mainly been used to purchase private land, whereas most informal settlements are located on government-owned lands.

Similarly, in Taguig the city has commenced a socialised housing programme, but again the households taking advantage of this tend to have members in regular paid employment. A number of households from informal settlements have rejected the opportunity to buy a unit because they considered they could not maintain the repayments at the level they are set at.[5] The local government also has plans to partner with an non-governmental organisation (NGO) called Coalition for the Homeless – established by 'former presidents of realty businesses' – to provide dwellings for local government employees, police and teachers, but this again excludes the poorest households.[6]

Another NGO active in Taguig, *Gawad Kalinga*, is a middle-class movement which provides donated housing to the poor, often through corporate social responsibility schemes. The movement, whose name means 'extending care', was first established as an off-shoot of the evangelical group, Couples for Christ. Its founder connects poverty alleviation to personal transformation in direct, intentional contrast to the confrontational style of community organising which has characterised progressive movements in the Philippines for a number of years (Kessler and Rüland, 2008: 194–5). Although it is now independent, *Gawad Kalinga* retains the same strong commitment to change through relational, personal transformation. *Gawad Kalinga* personnel articulate their priority as 'bridging the gap in relationships [in Philippine society] with "care and share"'.[7] The application of this approach to slum eradication has been popular with middle-class Filipinos; however Pinches suggests that part of the appeal is the way that it taps into 'an old and powerful discourse of paternalism enunciated by the Church, by members of the elite, and by politicians ... rendering the super-ordinate party active and generous, and the dependent other compliant and grateful' (Pinches, 2010: 205).

Overall, then, to date efforts by these local governments to fulfil their legal responsibilities to provide housing for the poor have been patchy and have not addressed the problems of the poorest households. The ADB scheme, then, would seem to fill a clear gap in provision. However, local governments in Metro Manila did not agree to the programme with the result that it failed to be implemented. Arguably, this was because mayors identified their interests with a quite different model of development. As Shatkin (2007: 36) points out, local government officials generally have a strong interest in commercial development of land within their jurisdictions, 'both because influential business people make powerful political allies, and because officials themselves often come from families with real estate interests'. Despite their legally mandated role to provide housing for the poor, class and political alliances prompted mayors to prefer and compete over 'commercial development, industrial development

and high-value residential development, as well as the development of public buildings such as colleges, hospitals or government
offices' (Shatkin, 2007: 36). Such developments deliver high revenues
through property and business tax, in a context where local governments have been given greater responsibility for service delivery under
decentralisation. For local governments in Metro Manila, business
and property taxes now constitute a larger share of revenue than the
Internal Revenue Allotment awarded to them by the national government (Shatkin, 2007: 36).

This prompts mayors to espouse a quite different view of development than that envisaged by the ADB. The weakness in the ADB's
plan was the assumption that local governments would commit
to a plan to deal with 'the informal settler problem' in ways that
would enable higher value commercial developments *and* the socio-
economic inclusion of poor households. This was not the case. The
ADB requirement that housing subsidies be derived from the local
government's continued ownership of the land meant that, for
mayors, that area was lost to higher value returns. Although the local
governments never really mobilised in opposition to the scheme,
this was in large part because, as gatekeepers, they did not need to do
so. The ADB could not pressure them to take the loan and there are
few costs in refusing. The local governments were well disposed to
taking on ADB loans in general, just not for the purpose of addressing urban poverty in the manner proposed by the ADB.

In this situation, the question arises whether working politically
could have transformed the mayors from wreckers of the plan to
opportunistic supporters of it. The scheme aimed to 'incentivise'
local government to take part,[8] but the funds and technical assistance
were not sufficient. On the other hand, studies of urban housing in
Metro Manila suggest that advances are made when the urban poor
themselves lobby their elected representatives for change. To quote a
major international development consultancy, there is 'a long history
of successful engagement with communities in slum upgrading' in
Metro Manila (GHK, 2011: 52). However, the ADB did not attempt to
work directly with effected communities to mobilise support for its
scheme. Some NGO personnel were hired to undertake community
surveys, but nothing more. The advocacy NGOs with experience in
community organising and pragmatic demand-making were largely
kept uninformed and uninvolved as planning proceeded.

Whilst the point of the programme was to finally upscale slum upgrading to a city-wide level, the invariably site-specific nature of the interventions in each local government area could have been the setting for familiar political struggles. But it is in fact unlikely this would have involved an easy convergence of urban poor household interests with the ADB programme because, whilst community leaders considered what was on offer was very attractive – 'no doubt about it, it is beautiful, like condominiums, with parking lots, playgrounds' – they considered it unaffordable.[9] So long as the ADB would not compromise on its idealist position regarding the technical aspects of its plan, there was no space for tactical or pragmatic engagement.

Participatory budgeting in Mataram: idealism in retreat

As discussed in the previous chapter, Mataram has been regarded as a showcase for post-authoritarian civic engagement in Indonesia with a variety or reformist groups taking part in spirited contestation of new modes of governance and distribution of power, based on idealist rhetoric. Participatory forms of development have been promoted in the country, as elsewhere, to provide political space for such engagement, and idealist reformers in Mataram were closely involved in establishing these. However, ideological differences among reformers, combined with the co-option of key reformers into the new money politics characterising post-Soeharto Indonesia, ensure that participatory budgeting achieved unimpressive results.

The first efforts to invite civic involvement in planning processes in Indonesia occurred in 2000, with donor assistance, specifically from a United Nations Development Programme project and the World Bank. Scholars at Mataram University, local legislators and civil society organisation (CSO) activists collaborated in designing a community forum, *Musyawarah Pembangunan Bermitra Masyarakat* (*MPBM* or Community Partnerships Development Forum), intended to facilitate consultation for sustainable urban development in Mataram and enhance public participation in local development projects. *MPBM* provided multiple forums for deliberation over development planning, from the grass-roots level to the municipality. The programme focused on ensuring that different communities in Mataram's multicultural population were represented and enabled to articulate their interests (Hidayatulloh, 2003: 62–63). *MPBM* was followed in 2002 by a programme called Community Action Plan, introduced by a local consultancy network and supported and funded by the German development agency. This programme uses a participatory planning approach to bring government officials and citizens together to identify problems and solutions in the economic sector. It is held at the village level and the results have been adopted as part of annual development plans by the Mataram municipal authority.

Two years later, the national government formally institutionalised the multi-level deliberative forums in every district to develop annual, medium and long-term plans for development known as *Musyawarah Perencanaan Pembangunan (Musrenbang)*. Then, from 2007, a new state-driven participatory forum supported by the World Bank, called the *Program Nasional Pemberdayaan Masyarakat* MANDIRI, was established to enhance poverty alleviation efforts. The proliferation of these processes suggests that both central government and donors see them as useful governance devices.

CSOs in Mataram were active in building a coalition of activists for budgeting that included various influential religious organisations such as *Nahdhatul Wathon, Muhammadiyah* and *Nahdlatul Ulama*, as well as journalist organisations and academics. The coalition established a 'Budget School' to educate citizens about the public budget and the need for transparency. Meanwhile another advocacy network of journalists, funded by The Asia Foundation and the Ford Foundation, developed alternative media for publicising information about anti-corruption campaigns and public budgeting. This journalist community subsequently became the 'embryo' of an organisation called the *Aliansi Jurnalis Independen* of West Nusa Tenggara. Still another network of 13 organisations joined with some provincial lawmakers in West Nusa Tenggara to create an alliance for public advocacy, engaging in activities from awareness-raising to investigations of abuses to boycotting parliamentary meetings.

Clearly, Mataram was fertile ground for idealist and pragmatic reformers interested in participatory budgeting. However, as discussed in Chapter 5, the results were less than impressive; these reformers were ultimately unsuccessful in wresting control of budgeting from bureaucrats operating via the usual mechanisms of money politics in Indonesia. There were three groups of reformers particularly evident in the city: civil society activists, who included not only NGOs but also journalists associations and academics; lawmakers; and reform-minded bureaucrats, all who were spread over idealist and pragmatic reformer camps. However, in each case, these reformers were outnumbered locally by more traditional actors, and were unable to gain sufficient independence from the traditionalists to make their campaigns count. Examining the reasons for this requires a closer analysis of the weak nature of CSOs and their political strategies in Mataram.

CSOs have become more numerous in Mataram since the end of the New Order era, but they are not particularly strong. Whilst they benefited from the weakening of central authority and the emergence of a new commitment to rights, freedoms and democracy, they were not in a position to reorient to the new conditions as quickly and effectively as did local elites. When attempting to confront local bureaucrats and politicians over issues of budgeting, CSOs were thus on the back foot.

First, the long period of repression under Soeharto meant that civil society groups lacked both experience in political lobbying and mobilisation and a grass-roots base (Antlöv, 2003: 75). NGOs tended to be reliant on international funding, and consequently their programmes were closely oriented to international rather than local approaches and ideals. Furthermore competition for such funding tended to pit NGOs against one another, putting pressure on NGO alliances.[10] Hence, in an attempt to extend their influence within the community, reformist NGOs formed pragmatic alliances with traditional organisations, such as religious ones, as a means to gain access to and credibility within poor communities. This pragmatism was successful only up to a point. Calling culturally strategic social actors to be part of the coalition was important because such actors offer important ideological support to the familiar, closed, hierarchical and patronage-oriented forms of governance that participatory budgeting was supposed to challenge. However, at the same time, it tied NGOs into a system dominated by links of patronage to political figures and by clientelist attitudes. This was antithetical to the aim of persuading villagers to stand up and demand a public reckoning from corrupt agents of the state in government-organised forums. Thus the NGOs found themselves in a catch 22 situation. Alone they were too weak and fragmented to take on the mighty Indonesian bureaucracy. In pragmatic alliance with entrenched traditional groups, they found themselves bound both to individual patrons and to modes of organisation that undermined rather than enhanced their capacity to challenge government.

For reform-minded legislators and bureaucrats similar constraints applied. Many within political parties and the public service had class, educational and political links to some of the individuals leading the NGO movement. These were middle-class individuals who had attended the same universities, and had been part of the student movement that brought down the Soeharto regime in the late 1990s. The experience of the *reformasi* movement created close ongoing ties among this generation of students.

Once the crisis was over, and a new regime, characterised by more widespread opportunities for elites to exercise power through decentralised governance emerged, the interests of ex-students diverged. Even within the NGO movement, many NGOs, including those led by former student leaders, are shifting from an activist to a technical role advising governments via schemes funded by international agencies, rather than mobilising supporters. For former activists within political parties and the public service, the powerful resurgence of money politics, whereby campaign donations are exchanged for government contracts, as an organising principle of electoral politics undercuts the potential for reformist platforms.

Corruption eradication is an important battleground for reformers in Indonesia precisely because corruption is central to the reconsolidation of oligarchy in the post-New Order era, at the same time as it is incompatible with liberal democratic and Islamic ideals of good governance circulating among middle-class professionals, the NGO movements and international funders of civil society. Because the issue is so highly politicised and so integral to different modes of governance, it is an area in which idealists find it difficult to find pragmatic alliances for reform, thanks to the continuing power of oligarchs and the way the political party system has emerged alongside them. However, as the tide of *reformasi* recedes, idealists find themselves internally divided and with insufficient support to be able to prevail, and there are few opportunists at local level in Indonesia for whom aligning with corruption eradication represents a significant tactical advantage.

Demand for good governance in Cambodia: opportunism triumphant

The World Bank's Demand for Good Governance (DFGG) programme in Cambodia, introduced in Chapter 5, represents an example of a programme in which opportunism was a stronger force than idealism. The result of this was a programme of minor projects operating in particular areas, some of which met their rather limited objectives but with only a marginal impact on the nature of governance.

As described in the previous chapter, the DFGG programme was introduced by the World Bank in Cambodia in the context of concerns for good governance objectives espoused by international donors and taken up in NGO and government policy documents. Central to these reforms was the issue of corruption, regarded as compromising public sector reform, service delivery and the business environment. The Cambodian government has paid lip service to these concerns in policy documents; for example, the update on the National Strategic Development Plan for 2009–2013 states: 'For [the royal Government of Cambodia], the elimination of corruption is a high priority because it is an obstacle to achieving its goal of sustained high growth by fostering private sector development in order to reduce poverty' (RGC, 2009: 17). Progress on implementation has been highly variable, however. Cambodia's overall performance with respect to corruption has been abysmal. In Transparency International's Corruption Perceptions Index, Cambodia ranked 157th out of 174 in 2012, equal with Angola and Tajikistan, a slight improvement on its 2011 ranking of 164th, one place below Zimbabwe (Transparency International, 2009).

The nature of corruption in Cambodia is closely connected to the political economy of efforts to achieve peace and stability over the past 30 years, and to the growth of the private sector as the foundation of politicised rural development programmes. The political model of neo-patrimonialism combined with predation, described in Chapter 5, that has elicited election wins for the Cambodian People's Party (CPP) and powered economic growth during the boom years, differs substantially from liberal prescriptions for good governance. The ability to elicit donations from businessmen and spend these on highly politicised development projects, specifically presented to the population as gifts from patrons that are expected to be reciprocated during elections, is dependent on the maintenance, by political party leaders, of absolute discretion over contracts, concessions and distributions of budgets. As such, it militates against the emergence of a powerful group of reformers within the CPP dedicated to the promotion of regulatory regimes that can preside over such functions as procurement, budget execution and development planning in the interests of transparency, fairness and efficiency.

Unlike in Indonesia, where governments were focused to concede to tough laws and an anti-corruption initiative after 1998, and where elected politicians pay lip service to anti-corruption ideals, in Cambodia corruption has flourished openly and without apparent embarrassment on the part of the government and elite. Indeed, the government had cracked down on anti-corruption movements reflecting the significance of corrupt relationships between the private sector and the government in the political success of the CPP. The Clean Hands Campaign in the mid-2000s is illustrative. The campaign was organised by the Coalition of Civil Society Organisations against Corruption (CoCSOaC), with funding from the US Agency for International Development (USAID). CoCSOaC organised a number of events including a million-signature petition against corruption, delivered to parliament shortly before the national elections in 2008; and a televised music and comedy concert held in the national Olympic Stadium in front of 50,000 people in 2009 to spread the anti-corruption message.

A political backlash came after the US Ambassador, Carol Rodley (2009), in the opening speech made at the concert, claimed that corruption cost the Cambodian Treasury $500 million a year. The government made strong statements condemning Rodley and the campaign (*AFP*, 2009; Campbell, 2009); one senior official suggested that Rodley would be perceived as having allied herself 'with the discredited views of the international pressure group Global Witness which continually engages in virulent and malicious campaigns against the Royal Government of Cambodia' (Hor Nambora, 2009).

The linking of the anti-corruption with Global Witness – an international NGO that was expelled from Cambodia in 2007 following its exposure of government connivance in forestry crimes, and whose local members have been violently attacked, effectively repressing protest over forestry issues – cast a chill over the anti-corruption movement. An anti-corruption law was finally passed in early 2010, following 15 years in the drafting process, perhaps reflecting a perception within government that both international donor and Cambodian public pressure were building on the issue. However certain provisions in the law – such as the article mandating up to six months' imprisonment for whistle-blowers making accusations that 'lead to fruitless investigations'[11] – seemed certain to render it ineffective.

The Cambodian government's stance on the corruption issue reflects the extent to which areas of governance relating to the key concern of the CPP – the retention of discretionary control over the disposal of Cambodia's natural resources – are off limits to would-be reformers. Similarly, other governance areas, such as judicial reform, which could impinge upon this imperative, have languished, along with sections of the public financial management reform programme associated with increasing the regulation of control over budgeting (Un and Hughes, 2011). The Cambodian government has thus typically acted as a wrecker of anti-corruption reform.

Why, then, did the World Bank's US$20 million DFGG project get off the ground? The programme was initiated in 2008. In a press release announcing the project, the Bank explicitly linked it to the anti-corruption agenda, remarking:

> Stimulating citizen demand for better governance has become a fundamental tool for more transparency and accountability in public affairs, and an integral part of the World Bank's governance and anti-corruption strategy.
>
> (World Bank, 2008c)

In fact, the DFGG reflected a part-pragmatic, part-opportunistic agreement between actors with ulterior motives. This included the World Bank, whose reasons for pursuing the programme were mixed. On one level the Bank is an idealist actor, aiming to promote neoliberal conceptions of good governance in Cambodia. However, there was scepticism within the Cambodia Country Office as to whether a DFGG programme would contribute much to this goal in the Cambodian context. The Bank pushed ahead because it saw a number of side benefits to the programme. A key motive was to promote the Bank's reputation within Cambodia, following a number of high-profile disasters, and to try to build better relations with Cambodian NGOs who had been increasingly critical of the Bank's activities. To the extent that the goal of the programme was to generate positive media attention, this can be considered an opportunist stance.

More pragmatically, the Bank envisaged some positive short-term goals of the programme, including reducing a long-standing and deeply entrenched attitude of distrust between the Cambodian government and civil society, and fostering 'a culture of constructive engagement that NSAs [Non-State Actors] would carry over to other contexts' (World Bank, 2008b: 13). Although the institutions selected are not directly related to the key areas of natural resource management and land in Cambodia, and consequently do not tackle head on the political economy of corruption that underpins Cambodia's contemporary political regime, they do, Bank officials suggest, offer opportunities for the government to experiment with new and more accountable ways of working. According to a Bank official who led the project in its inception phase,

> We know there are certain things that are off limits. For example, what has happened with PACT and USAID [ie. the Clean Hands Campaign]. It is not explicitly written but it happens. The government will make sure that line is not crossed ... We are trying to close the gap between what is theoretically possible and what is actually happening. Without pushing the frontier, we can do a lot that isn't being done. Hopefully the frontier will move, but we can do a lot of things up to the frontier that weren't being done.[12]

This evaluation was based upon a view that civil society in Cambodia, although clearly weak, could behave more effectively given the necessary skills. The World Bank commissioned a report into the capacities of Cambodian civil society and concluded that the few oppositional advocacy NGOs that exist, working in the fields of human rights, land and forestry, largely with the benefit of strong international backing, were outliers in a movement dominated by service delivery organisations that survived by keeping their heads down and never criticising the government at all. The World Bank considered that the latter group of NGOs might be encouraged to become more critical and assertive if given training in social accountability techniques, such as participatory planning and budgeting, the use of citizens report cards and customer user groups, while refraining from the more confrontational forms of public criticism or political mobilisation that put the advocacy NGOs in perennial danger.

The World Bank anticipated a risk that the government would acquiesce to the programme provided it remained marginal to key concerns and then move to neutralise it if it seemed to be mobilising citizens effectively and challenging key interests. Consequently, the Bank went to quite considerable lengths to ensure that key ministers, including the Prime Minister himself, had been fully briefed on the implications of the project.[13] Preparations for the programme included a high-profile launch in which the Minister of Interior and Deputy Prime Minister appeared on Cambodia television announcing the project.

However, despite these efforts, the Cambodian government did effectively ensure the marginal nature of the programme, through some subtle reinterpretations which indicated the limits to their acceptance of the Bank's objectives. For example, NGO participants in the project pointed to a difference between the government and the World Bank in translating the term 'accountability' in discussing social accountability techniques. While the World Bank preferred a colloquial term, the government insisted upon an invented, technical term[14] suggesting some concern to substitute off-putting jargon for language that can be readily understood by Cambodia's many uneducated poor.

Similarly, the Secretary of State of the Minister of Interior, in charge of overseeing the Project Coordination Unit that runs the DFGG programme, noted in an interview that, when translated into Khmer, the programme was called the 'Local Governance Project' rather than the 'Demand for Good Governance Project' because:

> There was some complaint about the title. The word demand means demanding, imposing forcefully. This is not really good ... So when the World Bank brought this project we changed the title in Khmer to Local Good Governance Project. In Khmer we would not accept this kind of demand.[15]

In fact, for the Ministry of Interior, the idea of creating partnerships with local development or service NGOs as a means to monitor the provision of services was regarded as a useful method of improving surveillance at a time when the structure of Cambodian local government was changing rapidly under the influence of decentralisation reform: 'civil society can help to monitor subnational councils, work with subnational councils at district and province level and bring more local knowledge.' For the Ministry:

> One of the main assets for Cambodia is that we have 2,400 NGOs. Now they have capacity – they are doing a lot more work. In remote areas, only those working with NGOs know what's going on there. Their work is complementary to Government.[16]

The Government saw the potential to use social accountability mechanisms as a prop to already powerful systems of grass-roots mobilisation associated with the provision of small-scale development programmes. The championing of the programme by the Minister of Interior is in line with this perspective. The Ministry of Interior is the lead Ministry for the government's broader decentralisation and deconcentration programme, and has taken the lead in experimenting with a range of other accountability mechanisms focused on newly formed subnational councils. This is crucial for ensuring that decentralisation serves the government's purpose of entrenching CPP party structures better at the local level, as a guarantor of continued ability to get out the vote in national elections.

However, this strategy did not include a rapprochement with critical advocacy NGOs working in key issues areas such as forestry, land and human rights. In a context where NGOs are highly dependent on external funding, the US$4 million available via the DFGG scheme offered an opportunity for the Ministry of Interior to cement its relationship with 'constructive' NGOs:

> We have a principle of constructive engagement – it is clear that those that are not supporting the government will not be funded.[17]

The World Bank to some extent reiterated this approach in its programme, which only supported projects which were put forward by NGOs in partnership with a state agency. Such projects were guaranteed to be marginal to the key issue areas at stake in any serious approach to corruption.

In taking this line, the World Bank modified ideas of social accountability in a manner that better matched the Ministry of Interior's perspective. The World Bank emphasised that social accountability could be useful in promoting a less confrontational 'partnership' between civil society and the state in Cambodia. Yet this is different from the experience of countries in Latin America and South Asia, where social accountability initiatives took the form of deliberately public performances, revealing corruption and abuse in a manner that was intended to be highly embarrassing to officials targeted. The World Bank's approach risks depoliticising social accountability, and thereby transforming it into a means by which NGO skills and citizens' concerns can be co-opted into a more effective form of the party patronage-based development that has underpinned the CPP's increasingly tight grip on power in Cambodia. As such, the World Bank was attempting to encourage NGOs into a position of pragmatic engagement with the Cambodian government, as opposed to idealistic opposition. However, the Cambodian government's interest in this form of engagement was marginal and weak, and was unlikely to translate into tolerance of greater accountability with respect to the governance of the key sectors of the economy.

For Cambodian NGOs who participated in the DFGG and the training programmes associated with it this created an acute problem. Most NGOs in Cambodia are reliant upon external donor funding. This already implies walking a pragmatic line between maintaining government tolerance for their activities, and maintaining a reputation both for political independence and for competence and impact in the eyes of external donors. However, in the field of anti-corruption initiatives, particularly if this began to impinge upon the hotly contested issue areas of forestry, land and legal reform, it was questionable whether there was sufficient political space to balance these contending concerns. NGO graduates from the DFGG training programmes thus questioned whether entry into DFGG-style partnerships with a government that sought primarily to elicit rather than share information would be beneficial to their organisations:

> What is the benefit for NGOs from this? There is no clear answer ... There must be consultation first, to figure out whether they [the government] are willing or not. If we start monitoring the budget, how they spend it, the relationship will be put into question. There must be clear points to say that if you do things in the good governance area and get some pressure from the police, or from the provincial governor, you can come to us, there is a mechanism, or something like that. Then again, getting information on government money is not easy and if we fail we will lose credit with the donors.[18]

Another graduate of the programme, who went on a World Bank-funded study tour to India to see social accountability in action there, commented similarly on the significance of the political environment in Cambodia: 'The Indian government is very democratic: because of full democracy, the level of threat is almost zero. People can say what they want to say'.

In Cambodia, by contrast, this interviewee suggested, most of the NGOs that were likely to have the capacity to implement social accountability work 'are working for advocacy for change within government, so the government is not happy to work with them.'[19] From the NGO perspective, the DFGG programme risked reinforcing the divide noted by the World Bank report and by the government between constructive and oppositional NGOs. The programme could only possibly work if it focused on marginal issue areas that would have few implications or spill-over effects with respect to the key issue area of natural resources. This is, in fact, what happened.

Urban informal sector governance in Jakarta: refusal to engage

Whereas the three issue areas discussed so far were areas in which international donors had some direct involvement, this is not the case with respect to the urban informal sector in Jakarta. There instead have been some efforts at reform by community-based organisations within civil society and, periodically, by some city agencies. For example, the Jakarta City Market Authority has pursued a number of programmes to move informal vendors from the streets and into market buildings (Wisnu, 2009).[20] However, according to the Jakarta Residents Forum (FAKTA), these programmes have been poorly designed, failing to take into account the street vendors' need to move around in order to follow the trade and not be confined to one location. Also, placed away from centres of activity, often in buildings requiring renovation, these markets have been unpopular with both the vendors and their customers. The high fees imposed for kiosks in the markets have been prohibitive also, with the result that informality remains more profitable (Wisnu, 2009). However, attempts at rationalisation remain a feature of preferred official strategies for the informal sector because this accords with an ideology of development in which development is equated with public order. Such reforms have been undermined by the wrecker stance of informal sector workers themselves.

The 2012 election of a new, populist Jakarta governor claiming a pro-poor approach raised hopes of a new political approach that could be more inclusive of the informal sector. However, despite on the one hand initially consulting widely with street vendor and residents associations, community leaders and urban poor groups, and on the other quickly introducing reforms that included the disarming of the *Satpol PP* (*Satuan Polisi Pamong Praja* or Civil Service Police Unit) because of its notorious use of violence against street traders, the new governor has failed to actually deliver greater secure space for the informal sector. Plans to develop social housing in certain slum areas, for example, have been hampered by the politics of land acquisition. Here party politics have played an obstructive role, with national elites wary of the governor's popularity and rumours of his presidential aspirations. For example, a Ministry dominated by political opponents of the governor's political party has attempted to undermine his position by stonewalling the release of vacant land for social housing that is close to sites where informal traders tend to concentrate.

Meanwhile, alternative plans better reflecting the needs of informal sector workers have been put forward by civil society advocates. As stated in the previous chapter, there are various sectoral organisations who have achieved some local concessions by lobbying on behalf of the informal sector. FAKTA in particular has encouraged informal sector workers to run for office at the lowest elected positions of formal authority in the administrative hierarchy – for example as Neighbourhood Unit heads. Such positions would give informal sector representatives greater inputs over the allocation of budget funds and space at local levels. However, even when lower level officials are sensitive to the issues, priorities and interests of the informal sector, those higher up in the administrative system regularly get in the way of any reforms.[21] Where informal sector workers have been involved in *Musrenbang* (participatory planning) processes, of the kind discussed above in the Mataram case, they also complained that their participation was 'window dressing' used to legitimate predetermined agendas.[22]

The reality is, the informal sector draws its strength from being embedded in local communities, but this does not fit at all well with top-down institutional arrangements, nor does it with sectoral forms of representation through formal organisations, like unions or NGOs. The highly elitist orientation of state institutions in Jakarta, as in Mataram, has a stifling impact on the efforts of reformers to engage strategically on local issues.

Urban informal sector workers' reluctance to interact with state officials is another factor in the difficult reform context. For the very poor, interaction with authority is regarded as inevitably a losing game, and among vendors there is deep scepticism and hostility towards government, on the grounds it only serves its own interests and those of the rich and powerful. The recurrent experience of violence and eviction at the hands of the *Satpol PP* and local gangs has done much to destroy poor people's trust in local authorities and hence their openness to communication or dialogue. For many street vendors, the avoidance of state agents is a priority because they do not want to join the formal sector, or even have more equitable laws and ordinances introduced. Instead, they prefer to continue to earn their livelihoods, free from government control and official harassment.

Such attitudes – arising from a history of engagement with local authorities which overwhelmingly has been threatening – mean that generally informal sector workers themselves do not seek to advance reform agendas and programmes. The lack of a coherent or organised political lobby from the sector, either via sectoral and mass organisations, or representation via political parties, means that the struggle for urban space is conducted at the local level through ad hoc confrontations and accommodations and there is as yet very little impact on higher level policy-making.

Conclusion

The successful achievement of reform cannot be reduced to the existence or otherwise of exceptional individuals with 'political will'. Reform requires motive, means and opportunity. For reform to be carried out successfully, a reform alliance needs to exist, comprising individuals who have the interests (or motives) and the power (or means) to push through reforms. Furthermore, since development represents a decisive reallocation of resources, away from some group and towards others, an anti-reform alliance can be expected to form in most cases. Whether reformers have the opportunity to prevail depends on the relative distribution of material and ideological power between pro-reform and anti-reform alliances.

Our case studies illustrate reformers are not all animated by the powerful desire to 'get to Denmark'. In fact, such a desire appears rather rare. Instead we find a mix of idealists, pragmatists and opportunists, whose interests in reform are based upon different kinds of concerns. Consequently, reform alliances tend not to be stable. Instead, the attachment of different groups to the alliance fluctuates. For a reform to be initiated at all suggests a significant alliance of interests. But if key power-holders jump off the bandwagon at an early stage, due either to changing circumstances, or to the fact that their interest wanes once early goals have been achieved, then the alliance may founder. In Mataram, a high level of reformist interest in the early post-Soeharto years weakened once the new regime consolidated and new institutional realities loomed larger than old student movement relationships. In Cambodia, an opportunist alliance was sufficient to initiate a set of experiments, but there was little interest on the part of any of the reformers in taking this further into the dangerous territory surrounding issues of corruption and natural resources.

Three further conclusions regarding reform alliances also arise from these case studies. First, the nature of state institutions is highly relevant. In all three countries in Southeast Asia, reformers have to deal with highly politicised state apparatuses. In Cambodia, the state is heavily intertwined with the structures of the political party – indeed, is supported by these. In Indonesia and the Philippines, despite the fact that the political regimes offer more substantive rights and freedoms, the links between political actors, bureaucrats and business groups are close and often corrupt, strictly limiting the possibilities for the poor to use state institutions to achieve reform. Second, however, it is also evident that alliances have different degrees of power at different levels of politics. Urban informal sector workers have the potential to engage successfully in struggles for reform at the very local level, but experience of ill-treatment and defeat leads them to strategies of avoidance rather than reform when dealing with higher level officials. Reformers in Cambodia had some success with small-scale projects, but this could not be translated into root-and-branch reform.

The third conclusion is that, for reformers ideas about development matter as much as financial incentives. For mayors within Metro Manila, a scheme that the ADB regarded as financially sound looked like an unsustainable risk, because of a more negative assessment of the urban poor's potential for successful entrepreneurship and their effect on the overall investment climate. Similarly, the considerable positive contribution made by the urban informal sector in Jakarta to the city's economy, particularly in times of economic crisis, has been largely ignored by successive city administrations, due to strong ideological attachment to ideas about development as modernisation. In both cases, ideologies that privilege capital – rather than labour-intensive – approaches to urban development reflect the relative power of large property developers as opposed to informal sector workers. But this power is translated through development ideals put forward consistently by public officials, rather than converting directly into corrupt material interest. Such ideologies of development provide a rationale for public officials to equate public interest with the interest of the elite, again undermining the ability of the poor to gain concessions. In Mataram, reformist ideals emerging from the student movement were apparently stifled by the resurgence of money politics, as reformers within the legislature and bureaucracy found their reform efforts continually blocked and eventually concluded that self-interest was better served by conformity rather than continued rebellion. Meanwhile, in Cambodia, the Ministry of Interior puts forward an ideal of hierarchical and paternalistic government which undermines the democratising import of demand for good governance programmes and, indeed, of decentralisation more widely. The interplay between ideological and material factors, and the influence of this on reform alliances, has been insufficiently acknowledged in the thinking of international aid agencies about reform.

7
Working Politically: Understanding Alliances

Introduction

Rethinking governance reform in the manner proposed in the preceding chapters suggests that, for donor agencies, 'working politically' requires a reconceptualisation of aid programmes as limited interventions in ongoing development processes, plus a more nuanced understanding of putative 'partners'. How does this approach fit with, or depart from, the major shifts in international aid policy and practice articulated over the last ten years? This chapter addresses this question.

Innovations in modalities such as the Poverty Reduction Strategy Papers and, subsequently, developments arising from the United Nations (UN) Millennium Summit – the 2002 Monterrey Consensus and high-level Organisation for Economic Co-operation and Development (OECD) for a on aid effectiveness in Paris (2005), Accra (2008) and Busan (2011) – all focused on moving on from the bitter legacies of donor-set conditionality and replacing this with ideas about 'ownership' and 'partnership'. But, from a structuralist perspective, country 'ownership' is not achievable because national consensus is unlikely to emerge, due to the structurally conflicting positions of different classes within the national political economy. Therefore, donor agencies need a stronger appreciation of how they should relate to other political actors in specific aid contexts.

In this study, we use the term 'alliances' to describe donor relations with recipient governments or non-governmental organisations (NGOs). The key difference between alliances and the donor ideal of 'partnership' is that alliances are forged with actors who represent class rather than national interests, and who are therefore engaged in perpetual relations of opposition and struggle with other class interests within and beyond the borders of the state. Understanding donor relationships as alliances immediately calls attention to the political nature of the donor enterprise. Donors do not stand above the political fray, but enter it. The actors to whom donors transfer resources are politically situated and engaged with struggle against other class-based groups. Funding them is therefore a political act.

This chapter presents a typology of collaborative versus controlling alliances that donors might consider in 'working politically' to achieve incremental, concrete improvements in the standards of living of the poor. This typology builds on that for reformers in the previous chapters and, again, is illustrated through our case studies in Cambodia, Indonesia and the Philippines.

Donors working politically

For donor agencies, working politically is generally understood as funding participatory processes designed at uncovering the nature of development as a public good – an uncontested technocratic reality. It means incentivising, training or promoting particular actors who might be in a position to promote a particular solution. The problem is that in every country there are not only diverse but conflicting conceptions of the good. Furthermore, elites and subordinate classes have contradictory interests that often cannot be reconciled into the language of common good over the long term, even though particular groups within different sections of society may at times converge on common goals in the short term.

To an extent, this has been acknowledged by the sometimes radical language of the aid effectiveness agenda. The 2005 Paris Declaration on Aid Effectiveness, called for recipient countries to take 'effective leadership over their development policies and strategies'. Furthermore, 'ownership' of such strategies was to be ensured by means of 'broad consultative processes' through which governments would ensure that development strategies reflected a broad swathe of public opinion. This approach was presaged in the UN Secretary General's report on the 2002 Monterrey Conference on Financing for Development which states: 'governments must build within their countries – both developed and developing – the public support necessary to translate their collective vision into action' (UN, 2002: 5).

This attempt to integrate domestic politics into aid planning is intended to resolve the problem of inadequate political will that has plagued donor-driven efforts at governance reform. The view is that, if governments commit themselves to particular goals through processes of public consultation, then their own populations will hold them to account for subsequent lapses. Donors are required to help build capacity for governments to conduct the necessary consultations to feed into planning processes. This approach opens up the question of politics but does not fully engage with the conflict inherent in development processes. It significantly underestimates the stakes inherent in the ideological and material conflicts that are already ongoing with respect to development planning and the well-established strategies that elites use in order to defuse and derail such popular demands. It further assumes that populations will be able to articulate and defend a coherent development policy once given a consultative forum in which to do so (Booth, 2012).

In our analysis, the politics of implementing development strategies is less about holding government accountable for its (lack of) progress towards agreed goals, and more about ongoing trials of strength between different alliances of actors who pursue fundamentally different goals. 'Consultation' as a technical fix for the problem of politics cannot deliver national consensus. At best it can offer a superficial legitimising process for elite interests that to some extent accommodate the concerns of other classes. This analysis has three major consequences for donors.

The first is that while donors do need to take their lead from domestic actors, they should be wary of assuming that the elite speak for the nation. On the contrary, it is important for donors to gauge which sections of society in fact support a particular reform, and which sections oppose it, to assess the range of likely responses. Supporters of particular donor programmes may include the poor, the middle class or a fraction of the elite in a situation of conflict. Middle-class groups can mobilise the poor and help make their struggles more effective, although they can also be co-opted by the elite – and indeed by donors. The poor themselves may be able to cause some kind of disruption, either through protest action or simply through their modes of existence and, hence, 'quiet encroachment ... on the propertied and powerful in order to survive and improve their lives' (Bayat, 2000: 545). The response of elites to these challenges may be repressive or accommodatory, offering concessions to secure a tactical advantage or simply to make the problem go away.

The second consequence for donors is that 'ownership' is not necessarily long-lasting. Political struggles entail that contenders are continually reacting to changing environments and to their opponents' strategies and protests. This means that interests and tactics are recalibrated constantly. As a result, donors need to think about 'ownership' less in terms of something that emerges from a legitimate political process, and more as something that is adopted as a tactic on the part of an elite seeking to prevail over contending forces. It may be pro-poor if elites are in accommodating mood; it may be anti-poor if elites feel they can get away with being predatory. But it is never going to be disinterested or based upon a national consensus.

The third consequence is that 'ownership' is ideological. Elite dominance is based not only upon material power but also upon ideological power. In the contemporary world, the requirement to maintain ideological coherence implies the need for national elites to clothe strategies for retaining power in a variety of tropes, which may include the rhetoric of solidarity and national or regional identity, democracy and human rights, and/or property rights and GDP growth. Such rhetoric promotes the cohesion of elite-supporting coalitions, but also requires elites to make compromises and to accommodate popular ideas or the aspirations of rising classes. The strategic rhetoric emerging from elite groups reflects the political work that national elites do to ensure that the policies they elect to 'own' will serve them rather than undermining them. The relationship of such strategic rhetoric to elites' broader ideological position and to both their immediate and their long-term interests needs to be understood in order to gauge the strength and conditions of elite commitment to particular agendas.

In the light of these points, what are the implications for the strategies and tactics of donor agencies? Of course it is recognised that donors always balance objectives aimed at poverty reduction with other interests, not least with preserving those forces that suit broader strategic, political, commercial and ideological needs of donor countries and their governments. However, to the extent that the more pressing development objectives are concerned, the following points are salient. Whilst donors need to look for opportunities to work constructively with the local actors they wish to support, they should understand both the scope and the limits of the opportunities they find. This implies moving away from an uncritical understanding of every relationship as a 'partnership' and instead having clear means of assessing the level of commitment on each side, and what this implies for the level of ambition and the time frame of the programme. By commitment, we do not simply mean the degree of 'progressiveness' offered by various groups but the level of political resources and cohesion they bring. As we have noted earlier, 'progressive' forces often do not have the political muscle to achieve their ambitions.

Taking this approach also implies a radical shift away from the institutions-and-mechanisms approach of the past ten years, and towards an incremental approach focused on concrete problems and their solutions. This allows donors to take ownership seriously. Rather than seeking local support for broad, generic programmes that reflect expert prescriptions of 'best practice', or seeking out so-called 'champions' of development, donors may be more successful if they focus on specific reforms and base provision for solutions on an analysis of how the target constituency interacts with specific structures of power.

This means, in working politically, donor agencies will have to spend less time designing, piloting and scaling up programmes which engage the poor on donors' terms, and more time interacting with both the poor and with other reformer groups, including elite groups, in their own associations, their own spaces and on their own terms, with a view to constructing alliances. This can often require donors to reaffirm commitment to human rights and political freedoms, and to back this up with diplomatic action. This, of course, may be uncomfortable or even impossible where 'development' advocates within the donor country governments are subordinate to those elements with other strategic or commercial priorities. Finally, donors will need to compromise on their idealistic reform agendas and accept 'good enough' measures to improve the lives of the poor (Grindle, 2004b, 2007).

To summarise, donors should not expect to transform a situation that is in large part determined by structural imperatives. In other words, seeking and finding progressive allies may lead nowhere where they are politically marginal forces. Nevertheless, it is possible to work within the existing social order to obtain tangible improvements for poor and marginalised groups. Doing so, however, requires that donors adopt a different mode of aid programming, which is more responsive to shifts in local constellations of forces, and a mode of analysis that enables them to identify when particular forces line up in a manner that is favourable to change.

Disaggregating alliances

As a result of working more politically, donors may expect to enter into a greater diversity of relationships with a greater array of actors. In the same way as reformers can be categorised as dedicated or tactical, so alliances formed to achieve particular policy goals can also be categorised in this way, with varying degrees of formality and with different distributions of power. Where power is relatively equally distributed, these alliances are characterised as collaborative and where power is relatively unequally distributed, they are characterised as controlling or directive. These are summarised in Table 7.1.

Formal, dedicated collaborations represent the kind of 'partnership' envisaged in the Accra Agenda. We find such alliances when NGOs and political parties join coalitions or umbrella organisations to pursue goals to which both are ideologically committed, and in which roles and responsibilities are negotiated via formally constituted processes, such as monthly meetings. Long-term funding relationships between international donors and local agencies fall into this alliance category in some circumstances, for example, budget support from

Table 7.1 Typology of alliances

Collaborative (power relations are relatively equal)	Formal	Informal
Dedicated	Dedicated coalitions of like-minded allies	Networks of activists or elites
Tactical	Tactical coalitions, including coalition governments	Ad hoc movements and political deals
Controlling (power relations are unequal)	**Formal**	**Informal**
Dedicated	Cooptation	Clientelism
Tactical	Contractualism	Coercion

bilateral donors to friendly governments, or programme support from bilateral donors to reformist ministries. Similarly, solidarity relationships between NGOs from North and South might look like this.

Accra Agenda 'partnerships' are considered collaborative, post conditionality. However, the claims of equal partnership are not to be taken at face value. Donors do not always have the upper hand – as our case studies in Southeast Asia amply demonstrate – but we do note that power relations in long-term collaborative relationships can fluctuate from relatively equal to highly unequal, depending upon the circumstances. For example, collaborations turn more controlling when one 'partner' feels to the need to become more directive of the other over risks to their reputation.

Informal collaborative alliances between dedicated allies may take the form of networks. Instances include clandestine or loose activist movements, or 'old boy' networks that are based upon connections forged through school or university attendance or military service. Foreign donors may become involved in such alliances through, for example, their habits of linking up with officials in recipient countries who speak Western languages or have studied in Western universities, as in the case of so-called planning 'technocrats'. Such informal links may be significant in promoting particular conceptions of problems and solutions in a development context and, for this very reason, donors have seen them as a way to connect with reform 'champions'. Yet, such networks can lack an actual reform constituency and be politically weak as a result.

Tactical collaborative alliances form where groups see mutual advantage in co-operation over a specific issue or development problem, but for different reasons. Temporary political coalitions forming between environmentalists and farmers opposed to particular types of industrial development are an example, as are coalition governments established through deals struck between political parties that are ideologically at odds. Informal tactical alliances include ad hoc protest movements involving different groups and political deals struck through backroom negotiations. For donors, the tactical alliances of others may offer opportunities for projects to be implemented – for example, to mitigate the environmental effects of a development or to provide compensation and relocation opportunities for poor farmers facing dispossession. However, longer term donor support for such coalitions is unlikely to be successful due to the probability of interests diverging again, once circumstances change or if more far-reaching transformative programmes are attempted.

Donors may have their own tactical interests in pursuing such alliances. For example, bilateral donor support for and funding of a programme that provides business opportunities overseas for companies at home represents a tactical collaboration. Similarly ad hoc and short-term support for a particular group of NGOs not normally regarded as partner material, but who are pushing for a reform that donors believe is desirable, is an example of an informal tactical collaboration. Finally, in relation to elites, tactical alliances will in fact often be the best option donors have available politically, given the only marginal or circumstantial interest that elites have in reform. However, in such relationships, donors will again need to be alert to the uncertainties and trade-offs that are invariable involved.

Where alliances are based on unequal power relations, with one ally or a group of allies largely controlling the agenda, we can draw a distinction between four main types: co-optative; clientelist; contractual; and coercive. *Co-optative* and *clientelist controlling alliances* are formed when parties are dedicated to similar causes but their mode of engagement reflects the inequalities between them. Examples of co-optative alliances might include funding arrangements that are heavily policed by donors; or situations where one ally seeks formal control of the other, for example through vetting appointments or taking controlling positions on boards of management. Alliances characterised by intensive efforts by the stronger ally to 'build the capacity' of the weaker ally also fall into this category, particularly where capacity building incorporates an attempt at instilling or promoting particular values.

Importantly, to the extent that an alliance involves a more powerful, controlling partner, the dedication of the other weaker party to the goals of the alliance is something to be established rather than assumed. Weaker parties have strong incentives to appear to be ideologically on the same page as their donors, but this cannot be read as real commitment. Informal alliances of a controlling type include clientelist arrangements whereby the weaker party relies upon personal relationships with the stronger party for a flow of resources and protection. These kinds of relationships between bilateral donors and poor governments were very common during the Cold War, and although heavily criticised by aid specialists, are still common in relationships where foreign policy dominates the aid relationship.

Tactical controlling alliances include contractual alliances, whereby a powerful actor contracts or employs a weaker party to carry out a particular service, or invokes legal obligations. An example might be where a bilateral donor working with a recalcitrant ministry to provide a particular sort of healthcare hand-picks a few local staff for a project implementation unit, gives them a contract and pays them salary supplements in order to get the work done. Painful experience of the limited and tactical nature of engagement by local staff in such arrangements illustrates the difficulties of this approach. To the extent that an alliance involves a more powerful, controlling partner, the dedication of the other weaker party to the goals of the alliance becomes something to be established rather than assumed. Weaker parties have strong incentives to appear to be ideologically on the same page as their donors, but this should not be read as commitment. An instance of this is where NGO personnel are contracted to undertake certain programme tasks but are in fact not dedicated to the programme as designed. Informal coercive versions include relationships which rest upon some form of pressure brought to bear informally. Political clientelist relations between politicians and urban poor constituents take this form when exit is curtailed through threats of violence (Gay, 1998).

This typology is of course just a typology. In reality, alliances may contain many allies with fluctuating or mixed motives. However, the typology is useful in drawing analytical attention to the wide range of relationships that may be glossed over in project documents as 'partnerships'. It also highlights the kinds of things that would-be reformers need to know about the relationships they form with other actors, in order to assess how far the relationship is likely to travel, how ambitious its objectives can be and what kinds of issues might cause relations to break down. All of these factors will help to determine how much money and effort to spend on the alliance, and how much control over decision-making or resources to cede to one's allies.

In the remainder of this chapter we return to our case studies in Chapters 5 and 6 to understand how this typology of alliances assists in understanding the politics of reform in each case, and the way donors might responsibly engage in the light of this. In addition we cite other instances of aid programming – from Cambodia and the Philippines – which illustrate the potential of tactical alliances in support of the poor.

Southeast Asian case studies

The Demand for Good Governance programme in Cambodia was presented as a programme that served the long-term interests of all parties. In the typology presented here, it represented a programme for experimenting with formal alliances between the World Bank, NGOs, Cambodian government agencies and the poor, in the interests of promoting better governance outcomes. However, our research reveals that each of the groups that were involved in designing the programme – the World Bank, the Ministry of Interior and the NGOs – had tactical reasons for engaging which disguised their misgivings about the project.

The World Bank's primary motivation for the programme was to improve its image in Cambodia following a series of development disasters and to strengthen its relationships with both government and NGOs. At the same time, NGOs were keen to take up this opportunity, despite their scepticism about the potential for social accountability in Cambodia, because successful conclusion of a project with the World Bank would increase their prestige with other donors. The government was willing to go along with the scheme as part of its series of ongoing experiments in fine-tuning local governance, provided there was little risk of social accountability getting out of hand. This was achieved by limiting its scope to areas that were not particularly politicised and where civil society was neither well organised nor particularly assertive. Amongst the various discussions and project documents various mutually convenient misunderstandings arose which allowed the project to proceed but ensuring that it would not be transformative. The intersection between the tactical alliances of the government and the World Bank was very limited in this case, and stopped well short of any transformation of governance practices. The intersection of interests was just sufficient to allow the programme to get off the ground but prevented it from doing anything particularly ambitious that could have had a significant impact on governance processes.

In Mataram, similarly, an ostensibly participatory programme initiated in the aftermath of transition from authoritarian rule was quickly hijacked by bureaucratic interests that were able to regroup rapidly after the shock of the Asian Financial Crisis and Soeharto's fall. Although a dedicated informal reform coalition did exist that saw the process as an opportunity to push forward the interests of subordinate groups, this coalition was weak, with poor links to the communities they purported to serve. This reflected the legacy of three decades of prior repression of civil society under authoritarian rule. Ostensibly more powerful members of the coalition – those in the legislature and the bureaucracy – were faced with powerful co-optative pressures from within their own organisations.

The power of money politics is a significant factor here. Indonesia's fledgling democracy has emerged highly dependent on donations from business, both legal and illegal. Elected politicians find themselves hamstrung between the desire to represent constituents and the need to raise funds for their party's campaigns from investors who subsequently call in favours. Within the bureaucracy, also, long-standing alignment with elites in politics and business has produced a conservative ideology which thwarts reform ambitions on the part of junior bureaucrats, lures or co-opts them into corrupt practices and penalises those who rebel.

In both the case of slum clearance in Metro Manila and governance of the urban informal sector in Jakarta, outcomes exposed deeply held ideological positions on the part of city mayors and governors that reflect close alignments, and even long-term alliances, between city government and private property developers. In both cities there is an entrenched view that expensive shopping malls or exclusive gated residential housing schemes represent genuine development, while low-cost housing or work areas for the poor represent a step backwards into an underdeveloped past. This view is convenient for property developers interested in building projects with high margins and low levels of risk, and local politicians with at least an interest in earning greater revenue from property and business taxes following decentralisation, and often a political concern to foster powerful business allies.

At the same time, the weakness of organisation amongst the poor is a barrier to their ability to affect decisions. Although the poor represent a disruption to the visions of development shared by elite groups, they are generally not able to translate this effectively into sustained bargaining power over potential solutions. This is largely because urban poor organisations are very weak. In both countries, harsh repression under authoritarian regimes has been succeeded by a form of democracy which is driven by campaign contributions and under-the-table payments. Furthermore, in both countries there has been relatively little cooperation between organisations of the poor and those representing the middle classes. The latter have tended to regard the poor as problematic political partners because of their tendency to respond to populist rhetoric and vote-buying campaigns. Figures like Joseph Estrada in the Philippines, a populist president elected on a platform of helping the poor but subsequently indicted for corruption following protests led by middle-class groups, have polarised urban society in a manner that has associated the interests of the poor with the more seedy aspects of populism and consequently weakened their political voice (Hutchison, 2007: 867).

The Asian Development Bank (ADB)'s slum clearance programme in Metro Manila began with the understanding that tactical action was needed to encourage city mayors' participation. However, the programme foundered because it misconstrued the nature of the interests confronting city mayors, and the profounder, more dedicated alignments and alliances between mayors and commercial developers. Although the programme set out to 'incentivise' the mayors with loans and technical assistance, the prior embedding of local government actors in a set of long-term relationships with business interests and class-based visions of development was much too powerful, in both material and ideological terms, to be overcome by such means, and the incentives offered were far too weak. Importantly, the ADB avoided any tactical collaborative alliances with targeted communities, engaging with them instead via the NGO personnel formally contracted to undertake social surveys. Thus, the donor's political work to kick start the programme was limited to the authorities who were charged with its implementation, and therefore had formal 'ownership', but lacked the commitment to collaborate in any substantive way.

With respect to the urban informal sector in Jakarta, the various governors' attitudes to development reflect their long-standing alliances and powerful ideological positions rather than short-term rational choices or technical calculations. The previous governor's marked hostility to the urban informal sector reflected his embedding in ideologies of development and governance inherited from the Soeharto era of military dictatorship. By contrast, his successor,

Joko Widodo (popularly known as Jokowi), took on the governorship having a reputation as a reformer who is prepared to engage with informal sector street traders over their issues and not treat them just as a public order problem. However, Jokowi's reformist bent is not a simple matter of personal character; he has a very different, private business background in an export sector where bureaucratic interference represents a significant cost and so his interests do not obviously lie in supporting the status quo. Hence, his administration needs to draw its strength from public support through, for example, popular use of YouTube to publicise the recalcitrance of city officials. However, it remains to be seen whether this political strategy is sufficient, particularly if he seeks to rise further by standing for the presidency in 2014. 'Likes' on YouTube are difficult to translate into political power in the absence of organised constituencies that can raise funds, make representations, do deals and pursue a variety of other alliance-building activities. Jokowi's reformist inclinations have been tested already over land matters by government ministries with different political loyalties.

These case studies reveal the difficulties faced by reform programmes that aim to overturn long-standing and structurally embedded conservative alliances. In all three countries under discussion, the weakness of civil society and the power of money politics entail that subordinate groups face great difficulties getting reform on the agenda. Even where reform programmes are in place, as in Cambodia and in Mataram, they are unlikely to be particularly transformative. In Cambodia, the programme was politically neutered from the start, whereas in Mataram the strength and cohesion of the reformist coalition were eroded over time.

Examples of successful projects that take advantage of tactical alliances in order to benefit the poor can be found, however, in issue areas where the interests of the powerful embrace reforms that are genuinely transformative for the poor. In Cambodia, a European Union (EU)-funded project for reducing small arms and light weapons following the end of the civil war in 1998 took advantage of a particular set of circumstances to successfully reduce the number of weapons circulating in the country, with significant effects on public safety and, consequently, on social and economic activity.

The EU project contained a number of features that made it successful. First, it took advantage of a moment in Cambodian history when powerful actors were determined to enact reforms that would be transformative for the poor – namely, a rapid increase in security to be achieved by the immediate implementation of extensive gun controls. For the Cambodian elite, this was motivated by two major concerns: to reduce the amount of gunfire heard by visiting aid officials – particularly from Japan – at a time when the ruling Cambodian People's Party (CPP) was struggling to improve its international reputation; and to promote the 'strongman' image of the party's leader Hun Sen. Hun Sen and the CPP campaigned heavily on the claim that they had delivered victory in the civil war against the Khmer Rouge, and presented themselves as the only party capable of delivering and safeguarding peace in Cambodia (Samdech Hun Sen, 1997). Consequently it was important that voters should experience life as increasingly peaceful.

The programme also took place against the backdrop of a campaign to split its main political rival, the royalist FUNCINPEC party, from FUNCINPEC's own military network. This campaign had included a series of political assassinations of key FUNCINPEC military personnel in the period of violence between 1997 and 1998. A civilian disarmament programme would assist in ensuring that FUNCINPEC was unable to represent an armed threat. Indeed, the first efforts in this direction, conducted by the CPP themselves without donor assistance, were commemorated through the erection of a statue made of gunmetal from melted-down arms on a roundabout opposite the FUNCINPEC party offices in Phnom Penh. The statue took the form of a handgun with a knot in its barrel, pointing directly at the FUNCINPEC HQ.

When the EU project began, then, the CPP had already taken significant steps to improve security, through imposing better discipline on the armed forces in Phnom Penh and through weapon amnesties and destruction programmes and was already making political capital out of this. The EU extended the scheme, and was also able to push into new areas that had previously not been considered, such as better regulation of weapons by the military and better training of police in weapons-related matters. Consequently, the programme was successful both in assisting in accomplishing objectives of immediate benefit to the poor, and promoting awareness of possible next steps in military and police reform, even if those next steps were unlikely to be taken (SEESAC, 2006).

Another example, involving the ADB again, is more illustrative of potential rather than actual instances of a donor pursuing tactical alliances to improve programme outcomes for the poor. This is because, unlike the EU interventions in Cambodia, the issue area was one in which national and local authorities in the Philippines mostly had only a contingent, tactical interest in pro-poor reform. As a result, the ADB was quickly stuck 'in an invidious position between government and community conflicts' (Storey, 2013: 198), where its formal agreements and alliances were being infringed by implementing authorities but its more dedicated, ad hoc collaborations were highly risky as they necessitated political compromises to work.

Prior to its failed slum eradication programme in Metro Manila, in the late 1990s, the ADB supported the development of a resettlement plan for the thousands of informal settler households to be affected by the environmental rehabilitation of the city's major waterway, the Pasig River (ADB, 2008a: 27). From the programme's start up a few years earlier, there had been no such plan and, before its completion, over 900 households were pre-emptively relocated by order of the president, arguably to avoid the ADB's strict procedural requirements (ADB, 2008a: 32). After the resettlement plan was finalised and a multimillion dollar ADB loan was approved in 2000, there were further settler relocations to distant resettlement sites with no services and facilities such as power, water, schools and health centres (ADB, 2008a: 32). As a result there were a number of community confrontations with local and national government authorities, leading to several deaths. This caused the ADB to ask for a stay in the relocations 'until the conditions at the resettlement sites improved' (ADB, 2008a: 32). The ADB's interventions were not entirely successful, but they did further open the political space for affected communities to mobilise and secure various concessions from local and national politicians (Murphy and Anana, 2004): '[o]riginal plans were revised and some people's proposals were incorporated' (Marcelino, 2005: 123).

The Pasig River programme's core objectives were highly contested. From the outset, it received strong political support from all levels of government, but only as an environmental and urban renewal programme. Whereas the ADB considered the programme 'should have been mainly a relocation and livelihood restoration project', this interpretation was resisted by relevant authorities on the grounds that, as 'illegals', the settlers were not entitled to compensation because such payments would 'open the flood gates of misplaced expectations' and encourage further squatting (ADB, 2008a: 28 and 34). The ADB's stance over the resettlement issue saw affected communities and their dedicated NGO advocates seek to engage it in tactical alliances. But this meant the Bank was a part of political processes that it could not control, around demands that it did not always support. It preferred the route of consultations with affected communities; however, these were no substitute for the mobilisations which the poor and their advocates found to be more effective in changing the stance of several mayors. Urban poor rallies in support of deposed President Joseph Estrada caused his successor, President Gloria Macapagal-Arroyo, to declare a moratorium on relocations and even proclaim areas of private land for expropriation by the local government for social housing (Marcelino, 2005: 117–21).

The Pasig River rehabilitation programme entailed a clear clash of development ideologies and hence priorities. The ADB struggled to enforce its formal agreements and alliances with relevant authorities, but at the same time, there were 'few actual examples of formalized relationships and partnerships' involving the affected communities (Storey, 2013: 197), and certainly none to address conflicts of interests and complaints. Yet, precisely in such a situation, where a subordinate group is causing significant disruption, various targeted local and national elites have a tactical interest in offering concessions to make the problem go away. The ADB's interventions in funding the programme did alter the political dynamics involved, in ways that directly and indirectly assisted the affected poor, but it remained organisationally challenged in attempting to respond other than by the book.

Implications for donors

Examples such as these case studies show that there are opportunities to take concrete measures to transform the prospects of the poor, but that these are highly political. Many donor agencies, despite rhetorical commitment, shy away from getting involved in 'deeper' governance reform processes. The main reasons for their difficulty in engaging with politics, as described in earlier chapters, derive from the incentive structure and the development-oriented outlook that characterise donor agencies. These donor agencies may use political economy analysis to prepare their staff for working in aid-recipient countries, but will not use it to determine the design of their policies.

Donor agencies that are serious about the need for governance reform and wish to engage with the political marginalisation of the poor in developing countries may want to proceed on the road to political economy analysis, and actively apply the insights derived from this type of analysis. The concrete use of political economy analysis has the capacity to make aid more effective as well as more directly beneficial to the poor. The discussion in this book has pointed out that in many cases pro-poor policies require a critical attitude versus the ruling elite in developing countries, as their approaches tend to be quite harmful to the cause of poor and marginalised segments of the population.

The approach sketched in previous chapters would guide donors in searching for occasions when opportunities for reform already exist. This does not mean looking for idealist reform champions. Idealist reformers are easy to identify, but they are also frequently uninfluential. Idealists will be found in certain civil society organisations, and supporting such organisations through solidarity strategies may be the first strategy that donor agencies can adopt. Their activities would very likely be twofold.

In the first place, donor agencies can apply diplomatic pressure to try to secure political space within which civil society groups can advocate for the cause of the poor and marginalised. The objective of supporting such groups would be to enhance awareness among larger parts of the population of the living conditions and limited access of the poor, in order to influence policy-making in the longer run. In the second place, civil society organisations could be recruited for the implementation of programmes and project aimed at the poorest parts of society.

A more innovative and potentially more powerful use of political economy analysis, however, is to provide development agencies with an understanding of when political opportunism can be harnessed to the cause of pro-poor governance reform. Opportunists may be tempted to engage in tactical alliances with donors if their short-term interests run parallel with those of the aid agencies. Such a situation may exist when a specific part of the elite notices that its engagement with the pro-poor policies of the donors will enhance its own political power base among the poor. This could be true, for instance, for elites originating from the part of a developing country where many of the poor are concentrated.

However, in building tactical alliances with opportunists, donors need to think differently about the nature of reform programmes. These need to be designed not as a blueprint for wholesale transformation of the state but as a series of limited steps each of which delivers some kind of concrete outcome. Designing programmes in such a way takes advantage of political opportunism, while remaining aware of its limitations. Programmes which proceed on this basis can be easily suspended or cancelled when political motives have run their course or when changed circumstances reduce elite interest. Furthermore, programmes with this kind of modular design ensure that political work to establish the intentions, interests and concerns of allies at every step of the way. Such an approach builds in awareness that motivations fluctuate and that reform is necessarily contingent, contested and uneven.

The outcome of political struggles over reform has an impact on the political resources that pro- and anti-reform groups manage to mobilise. Consequently, donor agencies need to recognise that they are regarded by political actors in recipient countries as part of the political struggle, particularly if they act to support the space for idealists and pragmatists to contest powerful elite agendas. Committed donors will need to be prepared to support the cause of the reform-oriented pragmatists and risk a deterioration of relations with those at the helm of the state. When engaging with governance reform in developing countries, donor agencies may come under attack from domestic constituencies which wish to maintain 'good relations' with specific foreign regimes for strategic or commercial reasons. The need to navigate in rough waters both at home and abroad obviously requires that donor agencies can think and act politically, and both justify and persevere with their chosen strategies. The tendency of these agencies to minimise risks, as well as their relatively low place in the pecking order of foreign-policy making, are not the best ingredients for the assertive pursuit of development strategies. As we re-iterate in the conclusion, this is why most of the aid industry is on the road to nowhere as far as political economy analysis is concerned.

8
Conclusion: The Road to Nowhere?

Introduction

Our central purpose in this book has been initially to ask why political economy has emerged as a tool for policy analysis and planning within the major aid agencies and banks. These had for decades been resolutely opposed to consideration of the political and social contexts of development reform, clinging to the assumption that various policy and institutional fixes would be enough in themselves to steer development in the 'right' direction. Also, it has been our aim to explain the different ways in which political economy has been understood and applied by policy-makers. Thus, we have made a close analysis of rational choice political economy, institutional political economy and the more pluralist versions of political economy that do take into account factors of power and social relationships. We examine how these approaches have shaped different agendas for policy and strategy in more practical terms.

Most importantly, we develop a specific approach to political economy that stresses the essential structural relationships that entangle and define the relative power of reformers and conservatives alike. Through this lens, we argue that the mainstream political economy approaches possess fundamental flaws both in their understanding of the dynamics of development and in the lessons they offer for policy and practice. In this chapter, we review what we consider to be the key political economy constraints on the aid industry's attempts to work more politically. These make progress difficult, but it is also the case that there remain political opportunities.

Political economy of donor agencies

We make the initial proposition that any political economy of development needs to be introspective to the extent that it should dissect the ideas and interests that shape the aid industry within donor countries. At one level, this means sorting out the ideological disputes between the more fundamentalist of market approaches and others that take institutions and/or political interests and power more seriously. At another level, it means assessing the conflicts that arise between development agencies and their domestic constituencies, and those other elements within donor country governments that give primacy to commercial or geo-strategic priorities: those located in the foreign affairs or trade ministries, or within the corporate and business communities.

Development assistance policies are a part of the foreign-policy equation of governments. Foreign policy is generally understood as an instrument to further the strategic and commercial interests of countries, and development assistance can only escape from the foreign-policy parameters to a limited extent, as much research on the impact of 'donor interests', 'recipient needs' and 'normative ideas' on aid allocation has shown (see Clist, 2011). It is small wonder that decisions on development assistance are often guided at least as much, or more, by perceived geo-strategic and economic interests of donors as it is by their desire to 'do good' in the global South (Lancaster, 2007; VanderVeen, 2011). Moreover, the relatively low position of aid agencies in the pecking order of policy-making reduces their leverage in budget negotiations vis-à-vis other government departments which have a much easier job in justifying their activities in terms of the contribution to the national interest.

This is a landscape that does much to explain the limits and constraints that apply to any donor agency. But these are not the only factors. As we have explained in Chapter 3, the options for donor agencies are also shaped by various administrative and reporting processes and, in particular, the degree to which the new public management has come to define the agencies and banks is critical. Where new public management is predominant, agencies will tend to be terminals for outsourcing the design and implementation of programmes. Agency functions will be concentrated on the tender process, the selection of sub-contractors and the assessment and reporting of outcomes.[1]

Providing procedures and regulatory frameworks for governance and other activities more suited to quantitative assessment and reporting will be favoured. Moreover, in the words of William Easterly (2002: 228), donor agencies are in the business of 'moving money'. As a result of their mandate, staff incentives in the aid agencies are related, in the first place, to the disbursement of funds allocated to them for development projects and programmes. The everyday practice of donor agencies forces them to be more concerned with the implications of their 'logical frameworks' than with the environment they find themselves in. For donors, 'doing development' is, first and foremost, implementing programmes and projects.

Political economy of recipient countries

We have argued that the embrace of political economy by various donor agencies has generally meant they accept the usefulness of analysing the political landscape of recipient countries in order to identify potential allies – progressive forces and champions of development. Our main assertion here is that domestic political forces and social interests are always embedded in larger relationships of power. Throughout we have assumed that a useful way to determine power positions is by relating these to some sort of material basis – be it the ownership of capital, access to natural resources or command of the strong arms of the state. Existing governance arrangements work in the interests of the dominant power-holders, while subordinate groups are marginalised and generally fail to get access to the formal decision-making structures.

On this basis, one of the most important issues highlighted in previous chapters concerns the assumption that development can be regarded as a public good. In other words, that Pareto-optimal solutions to development problems can be found if donors, in cooperation with recipient governments, apply the correct technical instruments. Poverty reduction, as the main target of contemporary development polices, is thus presented as non-exclusive and non-rivalrous – something that makes everyone better off.[2] Even the political economy community of scholars, consultants and development practitioners, who pay far more attention political dynamics, consider development problems as collective action problems whose resolution benefits society as a whole (see Chapter 4).

Our contention throughout this book has been that development is conflict-ridden. The spreading of the fruits of development more generally – that is, to groups that have traditionally been marginalised and disenfranchised – requires a restructuring of the social order. The groups who have traditionally benefited from the existing order will perceive change as inimical to their interests, and thus will attempt to ward off reform. Conversely, it is often the case that progressive forces are on the margins politically. The small farmers who want land reform, for example, are often caught in large networks of debt and obligation that limit their capacity to press for such reform. The pluralist theory of politics, which sees the political process as an essentially benign struggle for power among groups, is insufficiently able to understand the difficulty of the marginalised and disenfranchised in getting access to the political arena in the first place. Governance reform, if seriously pursued by development agencies, will require these agencies to get enmeshed in the political struggles that result from the expected opposition of (parts of) the elite that do not wish to give up their privileges.

Understanding the insights from structural political economy can enable donors and reformers to be more strategically informed in their decisions. To begin with, such knowledge can tell donors and reformers what not to do. This is important. There have been numerous examples of where policies and programmes that make sense from a market perspective have actually consolidated the power of elites and dispossessed smaller players. While the privatisation of public land (including forests) and the issuing of land titles to small farmers might sound like a good idea, it has often led to land grabs by influential figures and their allies in government bureaucracies. In a World Bank rural land-titling programme in the Philippines, it was 'middle and upper class families' who submitted the majority of claims to have ownership rights (Borras, 2008: 68). Of course, concentration of land-ownership and wealth and removal of the poor from the countryside may be what some reformers want. But where this is not the case, some reforms may be undesirable, at least without prior reforms at the political level.

Understanding the structural relationships that bind various interests also means that some of the most effective alliances will be tactical rather than strategic. It is difficult to ignore or to confront powerful interests, including those within the bureaucracy, in key ministries or in the military, for example. While these can be highly effective allies, it has to be recognised that their long-term goals will generally be inimical to those of reformers. These are no progressive forces or champions of development, but may be the basis of alliances for specific and short-term goals where their immediate objective coincides with those of reformers. Of course, this is a tricky path for reformers. Such alliances are bound to be fragile and volatile. Donors trying to intervene in the problem of informal settlements in Metro Manila had their hands tied by keeping them clean through attempts to pursue dedicated relationships with relevant authorities. Entering the political cut and thrust of conflicts over urban land use would not deliver easy wins,nevertheless, the history of related struggles suggests there were some opportunities.

Political economy of policy compromise

As we have noted, the frustrations of trying to address development goals, especially where they have implications for the existing hierarchies of power and the systems that sustain them, have forced some development thinkers to consider ways of proceeding that are less ambitious, or even to work within structures and with allies that would seem antithetical to most development objectives. Thus, Merilee Grindle talks about 'good enough governance', whilst others (noted at the end of Chapter 2) speculate on whether reforms can be incubated within patronage-based, neo-patrimonial systems themselves rather than insisting on a new apparatus of 'good governance' and other political reforms. But the question is; who is expropriating who? A structural political economy analysis (PEA) can provide a basis for further investigating the limits and opportunities of compromise.

Taking an idealist stance generally will not work politically. Therefore, in policy – and indeed ideological – terms donors are required to consider compromises, based on an understanding of whose interests are being served. If poverty reduction is to be a primary concern, then the design and roll-out of aid programming will need to be more attuned to the declared interests of the targeted groups living in poverty. This is also a tricky course for donors. Because poor people's demands are generally shaped by the material and ideological contexts in which they defend their livelihoods, they are not always in line with expert knowledge and opinion. Just as the political economy of reformers and alliances requires donor agencies to be less dedicated, and more tactical and opportunistic, in their approaches to aid programming, so too we argue that donors need to compromise on what they are prepared to deliver in terms of programme. Some of the time, indeed, the best thing they can do is to take a principled stand on human rights to protect what political space the poor have to utilise.

Political economy of changing global contexts

Our book had not focused on changing global contexts for aid and development, but this is the final critical challenge. On the one hand, it is perhaps a hard fact for development practitioners and policy-makers to accept that the aid industry is becoming an increasingly marginal player, both domestically and on the global stage. For most developing countries, private investment flows well exceed those coming through aid. Matching – and indeed helping to drive this further – donor country governments have declared their joint intention to move from 'aid effectiveness' to 'development effectiveness' to focus more on development through enhanced trade and investment (Ryder, 2013; Kim and Lee, 2013).

This is atop of the new geopolitical landscape of rising powers and new country donors, plus the growth in private sector direct involvement in development programming (Ryan et al., 2012). Finally, relatedly, there is the 'new geography of poverty' in which most of the world's poor are now to be found in middle- not low-income countries such as China, India and Indonesia (Sumner, 2012; Sumner and Mallett, 2013). These countries have the domestic resources to make head way against poverty, but the domestic politics of redistribution then looms very large. All these elements converged in the example of Britain ceasing aid to India by 2015 to commence a 'non-aid based' relationship based on the promotion of trade and private sector investment (Mulholland and Burke, 2012).

In relation to these trends, if we look back over the past decade, it is clear that two factors have become increasingly important influences on the nature and direction of economic and social transformation in developing countries. One has been the extent of capital flows and the financial crises that often accompany them. We can add to this the current currency wars that have such a significant impact on the terms of trade of many developing economies.

A second factor is to be found in the dramatic spread of global governance that is now embracing almost all aspects of economic life. To an important extent, the fate of developing countries is being fought out in the negotiation of trade and investment regimes and in intellectual property agreements and agreements on health and food security as well as human and labour rights. The Doha 'Development Round', concluded at the end of 2013 with quite a meagre result, is but one example of the changed geopolitical landscape making a difference, but only to a point (Scott and Wilkinson, 2011). Some of the measures being pushed by the US have serious implications for the sovereignty of national governments where they collide with the interests of private corporations. Under the terms of the proposed Trans-Pacific Partnership, for example, private corporations can sue governments and oppose dispute settlement by private courts. The prospects for social policy and the pursuit of public goods in such a situation may be severely curtailed, yet this features little in the ideas and mainstream approach of the political economy community discussed in Chapter 4, for example.

Where does this leave the aid industry? One path has certainly been for development agencies to act as the facilitators of global governance, helping countries put in place the new arrangements for the governance of World Trade Organisation agreements, or to assist governments to put in place new legal or financial frameworks. Donor agencies are also engaged in producing their own private sector development strategies to promote growth in developing countries (see AusAID, 2012). And various donor countries have signed on to the recent Extractive Industries Transparency Initiative (EITI) since its launch in 2003. Hence, it is difficult for development agencies to avoid being swept up into the new global governance behemoths. But, again, the decisions here are taken within the donor countries themselves and the way their policies are decided may well marginalise the aid ministries, as discussed earlier.

Conclusion

Does the analysis in this book then leave us without any hope as to the applicability of political economy analysis as an instrument of reform in developing countries? The list of political economy constraints above does encourage a fair degree of scepticism; yet there is no reason to be entirely negative about the leverage of donor agencies and see political economy analysis as no more than an academic exercise. We have said that, if donor agencies do not go beyond rhetorical commitments to working politically, they are on the road to nowhere. The road to somewhere, we can only repeat, lies in donors grasping the difficult realities of development politics and examining political opportunities on the basis of the insights from structural political economy. Even if limited, there are various ways in which donors can intervene in the struggles and experiences of the poor and marginalised that are worthwhile. After all, the normative goal of poverty reduction remains part of the contested politics of aid programming and development.

Notes

1 Introduction

1. As we shall see, this approach characterises the 'Drivers of Change' approach developed within DFID. It is also to be found in the Developmental Leadership Program developed by Adrian Leftwich and Steve Hogg, and within studies by the Centre for the Future State, Overseas Development Institute and even the World Bank. These will be examined in later chapters.

2 Realities of Political Economy: The Elephant in the Room

1. Some examples of the use of structural political economy in analysis of the politics of markets include, Chaudhry (1997), Hughes (2003) and Robison and Hadiz (2004).
2. The view that institutions are both an explanation for political and social problems and a solution for them is a central theme in World Bank thinking. See also Bates (2006) and Levi (2006).
3. These include such figures as Museveni of Uganda, Rawlings of Ghana, Chiluba of Zambia, Muapa of Tanzania and Kibaki of Kenya.
4. It has often been the best remunerated and trained sections of the civil service, including in the financial ministries and central banks that have been at the heart of many financial scandals (see, for example, Hamilton-Hart, 2001). Yet, salary increases for civil servants as a means of reducing corruption are still seen by neoliberal economists as an effective way to change behaviour within the public bureaucracy (see McLeod, 2005). But this assumes a short-term rational choice calculation that ignores the role of corruption as cement for wider political and social relations. As Harrison (2005: 252) has observed, higher pay scales have simply fed into existing systems of clientalist and informal politics in many African countries.
5. James Dorn (1993: 601) of the Cato Institute has argued that, 'Democratic government is no substitute for the free market'. Hayek (1967: 161) himself saw the ideal market state as one that essentially guaranteed individual property rights and contracts, and that might not be a democratic state.
6. The opportunities to access Chinese development assistance and loans became, for example, the basis of Chad's refusal of World Bank demands that it restricts the use of its loans for development programmes rather than for arms purchases (Massey and May, 2006) and the continuing ability of Sudan to chart an independent course in economic and geopolitical strategy. Former World Bank Head, Wolfowitz, has expressed concern that

Chinese bank loans, particularly in Africa, could undo the objectives of debt forgiveness programmes introduced by the West by opening opportunities for further plunges into debt (Crouigneau and Hiault, 2006). In Southeast Asia, too, the surge of investments from China, Singapore, Malaysia and Taiwan (see Watts, 2006; UBS, 2006) brings quite different implications for the broader politics of governance in that region.

3 Development Agencies and the Political Economy Turn

1. Interestingly, Gibson et al. (2005: 148–9) did not find evidence in their research on the Swedish International Development Cooperation Agency (SIDA) that past project performance impacted on staff promotions.
2. This section draws on Schakel et al. (2010).
3. The overview of Drivers of Change country studies at the Governance and Social Development Resource Centre website mentions studies on: Angola, Bangladesh, Bolivia, Cambodia, the Democratic Republic of Congo, Ghana, Kenya, Kyrgyzstan, Malawi, Mozambique, Nigeria, Pakistan, Peru, Tanzania, Uganda, Vanuatu and Zambia (http://www.gsdrc.org/index. cfm?objectid=597A76DB-14C2-620A-2770D688963DF944#doc, accessed 19 November 2013).
4. Van Ardenne broadened the group of partner countries to 36; one of the criteria for selection was 'the quality of policies and governance in recipient countries' (Minister for Development Cooperation, 2003: 19–20, 32, translated from Dutch). Koenders selected 33 countries across three different 'profiles': countries with a focus on accelerated achievement of the Millennium Development Goals, fragile states and (near) middle income countries. The least-developed and low-income countries in the first group were required to have 'a reasonable level of stability and improving governance' (Minister for Development Cooperation, 2007: 38–9).

   The subsequent Minister for European Affairs and International Cooperation, Christian-Democrat Ben Knapen, in 2011 announced a sharp reduction in the number of partner countries to 15. Good governance, including democratisation, respect for human rights and the fight against corruption, has remained a criterion, together with six other criteria, such as the prospects for obtaining results, the level of poverty and the opportunities for the Netherlands to work on four 'spearheads': security and rule of law, food security, water, and sexuals and reproductive health and rights (Minister for European Affairs and International Cooperation 2011: 14–17).
5. At the time of the launch of SGACA, DMH was called the Department of Human Rights and Peacebuilding.
6. Personal communication with Wil Hout by a staff member of the Department for Human Rights and Peace Building (DMH's predecessor), The Hague, 15 May 2006.

7. The track record, which was designed in the mid-1990s to assist the Ministry with decisions on macroeconomic support, has evolved into an instrument to judge whether countries qualify for particular aid modalities. The track record consists of four clusters: poverty reduction, economic order, good governance and policy dialogue. The Dutch embassies score the performance of partner countries on two criteria per cluster (see Hout, 2007: 58–61).

8. Staff members at ECORYS Nederland, interview with Wil Hout, Rotterdam, September 2009. It is remarkable that two papers by DEK staff members (Harth and Waltmans, 2007; Waltmans, 2008) on the need for political economy analyses of the reality 'behind the façade' do not mention SGACA even once. Details of interviews and interviewees are included in Schakel et al., 2010: Annex II.

9. The similarity between Drivers of Change and SGACA is due, in part, to the involvement of Sue Unsworth, former Chief Governance Advisor at DFID, as a consultant in the process of setting up the SGACA framework.

10. In 2007, discussions started on the extension of the SGACA framework to make it applicable to fragile states. After his appointment in February 2007, the new Minister for Development Cooperation, Bert Koenders, had been placing emphasis on the inclusion of fragile states into the Dutch development assistance framework. The extended SGACA framework, which included a security component, was approved in September 2008. A pilot was done with the extended framework in the Democratic Republic of Congo and Burundi, but the revised SGACA has never been applied to fragile states because most SGACAs had been completed before the original deadline of October 2008 (Schakel et al., 2010: Annex III).

11. Staff members at ECORYS Nederland, interviews with Wil Hout, Rotterdam, September 2009; staff members/consultants at Clingendael Institute, with Wil Hout, The Hague, October and November 2009.

12. Staff members at ECORYS Nederland, interview with Wil Hout, Rotterdam, September 2009.

13. Senior consultant, telephone interview with Wil Hout, January 2010.

14. Personal communication with Wil Hout by a staff member of the DMH, The Hague, September 2010.

15. A good summary of the criticism has been given in Alexander (2004).

16. A new formula for calculating the Country Performance Rating was introduced in the 15th replenishment period of IDA (IDA15, from 2008 to 2011). This formula is

$$\text{Country Performance Rating} = (0.24 * \text{CPIA}_{A-C} + 0.68 * \text{CPIA}_{D} + 0.08 * \text{PORT}),$$

in which CPIA_{A-C} stands for the average score on the clusters on economic management, structural policies and policies for social inclusion/ equity, CPIA_{D} represents the average on the five components of the governance cluster, and PORT represents the assessment of portfolio performance (International Development Agency, 2007: 9–10). In earlier periods, a so-called 'governance factor' had been used to emphasise governance-related criteria in the Country Performance Rating (see Hout, 2007: 31–40 for a detailed analysis).

4   Development as Collective Action Problems

1. Examples include the Overseas Development Institute, Oxford Policy Management, The Policy Practice, Institute of Development Studies (IDS), Developmental Leadership Program, the Elites, Production and Poverty Project (Copenhagen), UN-WIDER, The Asia Foundation, etc. However, collaborative outputs have been published by donors, for example DFID-funded research by The Centre for the Future State and the Development Research Centre on Citizenship, Participation and Accountability (both at IDS), the Crisis States Research Centre (London School of Economics), and the Centre for Research on Inequality and Ethnicity (Oxford University).
2. Hyden refers here to the functionalism of Talcott Parsons. The influential publication, *An Upside Down View of Governance* (Centre for the Future State, 2010: 9), focuses on 'public authority' as the capacity to 'undertake core governance functions'.
3. The ongoing research into pro-poor active citizenship has continued to delve into the politics of collective action more strongly in relation to power relations rather than collective action problems (see Joshi and Houtzager, 2012; Gaventa and McGee, 2010). Thus here there is a more strongly *relational* conception of collective action and how it is shaped by ideology, historical legacies, the nature of alliances and tactics, and position within power relations (Hickey, 2009). We return to the distinction between collective action in relation to power relations rather than collective action problems later in this chapter.
4. Leftwich defines politics as 'all the activities of cooperation, conflict and negotiation involved in decisions about the use, production and distribution or resources' (Leftwich, 2007: 13) and as 'the pervasive and unavoidable (and necessary) activities of conflict, negotiation and compromise involved wherever and whenever human beings in groups have to take decisions about how resources are to be used, produced and distributed' (Leftwich, 2011: 1).
5. Wright (2000), for example, discusses the 'associational power' of workers which comes from collective organisation and is therefore weakened through division and fragmentation.

5   Understanding the Development Problem

1. Socialised housing entails some level and form of subsidy so as to meet the shelter needs of households which cannot otherwise afford housing through the private market.
2. Ministry of Interior senior official, interview with Caroline Hughes, Phnom Penh, July 2010.

3. Ibid.
4. Civil society activist, interviewed by Universitas Gajah Mada research team, Mataram, October 2009.
5. Civil society activist, interviewed by Universitas Gajah Mada research team, Mataram, July 2010.
6. This section on the informal sector in Jakarta draws on Ian Wilson's 'The streets belong to who?: 'Governance' and the Urban Informal Sector in Jakarta, Indonesia' in the policy monograph, *The Elephant in the Room: Politics and the Development Problem*, presented at a Murdoch University workshop, 13–14 December 2010.
7. Jakarta Legal Aid Foundation officer, interview with Ian Wilson, Jakarta, August 2009.
8. FAKTA representative, interview with Ian Wilson, Jakarta, August 2010.
9. Housing Urban Development Coordinating Council senior officer, interview with Jane Hutchison, Metro Manila, August 2009
10. Urban poor community organiser, interview with Jane Hutchison, Metro Manila, 2006.
11. Since 2010, the ADB's Involuntary Resettlement Policy has been incorporated into its Safeguard Policy Statement, at http://www.adb.org/documents/safeguard-policy-statement?ref=site/safeguards/publications

6   Analysing Reform and Reformers

1. Different states, and different institutions within a particular state, do nevertheless have different degrees of autonomy, depending on the extent to which state officials are successfully able to monopolise key functions through their professionalisation and or the extent to which they are able to forge alliances with wider non-state forces to promote their autonomy.
2. This is not to say that elite individuals never 'cross over' to support causes that oppose their class interests: they do, and may bring along considerable resources, however, in structural terms their power is diminished.
3. Previously, the ADB had sought to release its loan to the national government; however, after many meetings it failed to convince the Department of Finance that the programme was viable (ADB, personal communication with Jane Hutchison, 2009).
4. The significance of a national government programme is that the subsidy is not provided locally.
5. Interview with Jane Hutchison, Metro Manila, 2010.
6. Interview with Jane Hutchison, Metro Manila, 2010.
7. Interview with Jane Hutchison, Metro Manila, 2010.
8. Housing Urban Development Coordinating Council senior officer, interview with Jane Hutchison, Metro Manila, August 2009.
9. Urban poor community leaders, interview with Jane Hutchison, Metro Manila, January 2010.

10. Interviews with various civil society activists, Mataram, July 2010.
11. Royal Government of Cambodia, *Chbap Stey pi Kar Prachang Ampoeu Puk Roluey* (Law on Anti-Corruption), draft submitted to National Assembly, 24 February 2010, Article 41, author's translation from Khmer.
12. World Bank official, interview with Caroline Hughes, Phnom Penh, June 2009.
13. World Bank official, interview with Caroline Hughes, Phnom Penh, June 2009.
14. Silaka, interview by Caroline Hughes, Phnom Penh, June 2009.
15. Ministry of Interior senior official, interview with Caroline Hughes, Phnom Penh, July 2010.
16. Ibid.
17. Ibid.
18. NGO activist, interview with Caroline Hughes, Phnom Penh, July 2009.
19. NGO activist, interview with Caroline Hughes, Jakarta, Phnom Penh, July 2009.
20. Jakarta City Market Authority official, interview with Ian Wilson, Jakarta, August 2009.
21. FAKTA member, interview with Ian Wilson, Jakarta, August 2009.
22. Group of *Musrenbang* participants, interview with Ian Wilson, Jakarta, August 2009.

8 Conclusion: The Road to Nowhere?

1. This point has also be made in relation to political economy analyses by Fisher and Marquette (2013: 3), who argue that '[i]n the last five or so years ... PEA has moved away from largely donor-designed broad political analysis frameworks for understanding the overall political context in a given country, to largely standalone products, designed by specialist consultants or academics, for individual donor agencies, but sharing many common features (and designers)'.
2. This seems to be the implication of the United Nations Development Programme's work on global public goods, though this conclusion remains largely implicit, see Kapstein (1999).

Bibliography

ADB (2005) 'Technical Assistance to the Republic of the Philippines for Preparing the Metro Manila Urban Services for the Poor Project', PHI 38398, July. Manila: ADB, http://www2.adb.org/Documents/TARs/PHI/tar-phi-38398.pdf (accessed 27 February 2013).

ADB (2008a) 'Asian Development Bank's Involuntary Resettlement Safeguards: Project Case Studies in the Philippines', Special Evaluation Study No. SST: REG 2006–14, September. Operations Evaluation Department, http://www.oecd.org/derec/adb/47108497.pdf (accessed 4 November 2013).

ADB (2008b) 'PHI: Metro Manila Urban Services for the Poor Investment Program', *Draft Design and Monitoring Framework*, Project No. 38398-01, March. Manila: ADB, http://www2.adb.org/Documents/DMFs/PHI/38398-PHI-DMF.pdf (accessed 13 February 2013).

ADB (2010) 'Technical Assistance Completion Report: Preparing the Metro Manila Urban Services for the Poor Project', PPTA 4616-PHI. Manila: ADB, http://www.adb.org/sites/default/files/projdocs/2010/38398-01-phi-tcr.pdf (accessed 4 November 2013).

AFP (2009) 'Cambodia Denies US Diplomat's Corruption Allegation', *AFP*, 2 June, http://www.assetrecovery.org/kc/node/e17ed9f2-500c-11de-bacd-a7d8a60b2a36.0;jsessionid=A27605412C3639C3498E129E6B9645AC (accessed 1 September 2010).

Alexander, N. (2004) 'Judge and Jury: The World Bank's Scorecard for Borrowing Governments', in Social Watch (ed.) *Social Watch Report 2004: Fear and Want, Obstacles to Human Security* (Montevideo, Uruguay: Instituto del Tercer Mundo): 17–23.

Amsden, A., DiCaprio, A. and Robinson, J. (2009) 'Aligning Elites with Development', *WIDER Angle newsletter*, August, http://www.wider.unu.edu/publications/newsletter/articles/en_GB/05-08-2009/ (accessed 24 September 2013).

Anderson, B. (1990) 'Murder and Progress in Modern Siam', *New Left Review*, 181 (May–June): 33–48.

Antlöv, H. (2003) 'Not Enough Politics! Power, Participation and the New Democratic Polity in Indonesia', in E. Aspinall and G. Fealy (eds) *Local Power and Politics in Indonesia: Decentralisation & Democratisation* (Singapore: Institute of Southeast Asian Studies): 72–86.

Asian Wall Street Journal (1997) 'Socialist International', *Asian Wall Street Journal*, 18 December.

Aspinall, E. and Fealy, G. (eds) (2003) *Local Power and Politics in Indonesia: Decentralisation & Democratisation* (Singapore: Institute of Southeast Asian Studies).

AusAID (2007) 'Building Demand for Better Governance: New Directions for the Australian Aid Program: Position Statement and Program Guidance', December. Canberra: AusAID.

AusAID (2012) 'Sustainable Economic Development: Private Sector Development', Thematic Strategy, August. Canberra: AusAID.

Bardhan, P. K. (1989) 'The New Institutional Economics and Development Theory: A Brief Critical Assessment', *World Development*, 17 (9): 1389–95.

Bates, R. H. (1981) *Markets and States in Tropical Africa: The Political Basis of Agricultural Policies* (Berkeley: University of California Press).

Bates, R. H. (2006) 'Institutions and Development', *Journal of African Economies – AERC Supplement*, 15 (1): 10–61.

Batley, R., McCourt, W. and Mcloughlin, C. (2012) 'Editorial', *Public Management Review*, 14 (2): 131–44.

Bayat, A. (2000) 'From "Dangerous Classes" to "Quiet Rebels": Politics of the Urban Subaltern in the Global South', *International Sociology*, 15 (3): 533–557.

Bello, W., Kinley, D. and Elinson, E. (eds) (1982) *Development Debacle: World Bank in the Philippines* (San Francisco: Institute for Food and Development Policy).

Benequista, N. and Gaventa, J. (2011) 'Blurring the Boundaries: Citizen Action across States and Societies: A Summary of Findings from a Decade of Collaborative Research on Citizen Engagement'. Brighton: Development Research Centre on Citizenship, Participation and Accountability.

Booth, D. (2012) 'Development as a Collective Action Problem: Addressing the Real Challenges of African Governance', *Africa Power and Politics Programme*, Synthesis Report, October. Overseas Development Institute.

Booth, D. and Golooba-Mutebi, F. (2009) 'Aiding Economic Growth in Africa: The Political Economy of Roads Reform in Uganda', Working Paper No. 307, September. London: Overseas Development Institute, http://www.odi.org.uk/sites/odi.org.uk/files/odi-assets/publications-opinion-files/4965.pdf (accessed 13 February 2013).

Borras, S. (2008) *Competing Views and Strategies on Agrarian Reform, Volume II: Philippine Perspectives* (Quezon City: Ateneo de Manila University Press).

Boudreau, V. (2009) 'Elections, repression and authoritarian survival in post-transition Indonesia and the Philippines', *The Pacific Review*, 22 (2): 233–253.

BPS (2010) *'Hasil Sensus Penduduk 2010: Data Agregat per Provinsi'*, Jakarta: *Badan Pusat Statistik*, http://dds.bps.go.id/eng/download_file/SP2010_agregat_data_perProvinsi.pdf (accessed 14 November 2010).

Brinkerhoff, D. W. and Goldsmith, A. A. (2004) 'Good Governance, Clientelism and Patrimonialism: New Perspectives on Old Problems', *International Public Management Journal*, 7 (2): 163–85.

Buchanan, J. M. and Tullock, G. (1962) *The Calculus of Consent: Logical Foundations of Constitutional Democracy* (Ann Arbor: University of Michigan Press).

Butt, S. (2012) *Corruption and Law in Indonesia* (London: Routledge).

Camdessus, M. (1997) 'Asia Will Survive with Realistic Economic Policies', *Jakarta Post*, 8 December. 5.

Camdessus, M. (1998) 'The IMF and Good Governance', presented at Transparency International. Paris, 21 January, http://www.imf.org/external/np/speeches/1998/012198.HTM (accessed 27 March 2013).

Campbell, S. (2009) 'Reality off the Rails in Phnom Penh', *Asia Times Online*, 26 June, http://www.atimes.com/atimes/Southeast_Asia/KF26Ae02.html (accessed 1 September 2010).

Capuno, J. J. (2002) 'Philippines', in P. J. Smoke and K. Yun-Hwan (eds) *Intergovernmental Fiscal Transfers in Asia: Current Practice and Challenges for the Future* (Manila: Asian Development Bank): 219–82.

Carlsson, J., Köhlin, G. and Ekbom, A. (1994) *The Political Economy of Evaluation: International Aid Agencies and the Effectiveness of Aid* (New York: St. Martin's Press).

Carothers, T. and de Gramont, D. (2013) *Development Aid Confronts Politics: The Almost Revolution* (Washington: Carnegie Endowment for International Peace).

Carroll, J. J. (1998) 'NGOs Confront Urban Poverty', in G. S. Silliman and L. Garner Noble (eds) *Organizing for Democracy: NGOs, Civil Society and the Philippine State* (Quezon City: Ateneo de Manila University Press).

Carroll, T. (2009) 'Attempting Illiberalism: The World Bank and the Embedding of Neo-Liberal Governance in the Philippines', in W. Hout and R. Robison (eds) *Governance and the Depoliticisation of Development* (London: Routledge): 137–51.

Centre for the Future State (2010) *An Upside Down View of Governance*, Institute of Development Studies (IDS), University of Sussex.

Chabal, P. and Daloz, J.-P. (1999) *Africa Works: Disorder as Political Instrument* (Oxford: James Currey).

Chaudhry, K. A. (1997) *The Price of Wealth: Economies and Institutions in the Middle East* (Ithaca: Cornell University Press).

Chhotray, V. and Hulme, D. (2009) 'Contrasting Visions for Aid and Governance in the 21st Century: The White House Millennium Challenge Account and DFID's Drivers of Change', *World Development*, 37 (1): 36–49.

Clist, P. (2011) '25 Years of Aid Allocation Practice: Whither Selectivity?', *World Development*, 39 (10): 1724–34.

Cock, A. R. (2007) 'The Interaction Between a Ruling Elite and an Externally Promoted Policy Reform Agenda: The Case of Forestry Under the Second Kingdom of Cambodia 1993–2003', PhD Thesis (La Trobe University, Melbourne).

Colas, A. (2004) 'The Re-Invention of Populism: Islamist Responses to Capitalist Development in the Contemporary Maghreb', *Historical Materialism*, 12 (4): 231–60.

Cooke, B. and Dar, S. (2008) 'Introduction: The New Development Management', in S. Dar and B. Cooke (eds) *The New Development Management: Critiquing the Dual Modernization* (London: Zed Books): 1–17.

Copestake, J. and Williams, R. (2012) 'The Evolving Art of Political Economy Analysis: Unlocking Its Practical Potential Through a More Interactive Approach', Development Futures Paper, February. Oxford: Oxford Policy Management, http://www.opml.co.uk/sites/opml/files/OPM_DF_PEA.pdf (accessed 1 November 2013).

Crouigneau, F. and Hiault, R. (2006) 'World Bank Chief Hits at China Lenders', *Financial Times*, 24 October. 14.

Dahl-Østergaard, T., Unsworth, S., Robinson, M. and Jensen, R. I. (2005) 'Lessons Learned on the Use of Power and Drivers of Change Analyses in Development Cooperation', Review Commissioned by the OECD DAC Network on Governance (GOVNET): Final Report, 20 September. Paris: DAC Network on Governance (Govnet), http://www.oecd.org/dac/governance anddevelopment/37957900.pdf (accessed 11 February 2013).

de Haan, A. and Everest-Phillips, M. (2007) 'Can New Aid Modalities Handle Politics?', *WIDER Research Paper*, Research Paper No 2007/63, October. Helsinki: United Nations University World Institute for Development Economics Research (UNU-WIDER), http://www.wider.unu.edu/publications/working-papers/research-papers/2007/en_GB/rp2007-63/_files/78271658917560461/default/rp2007-63-revised.pdf (accessed 11 February 2013).

DFID (2001) 'Making Government Work for Poor People: Building State Capability', *Strategies for Achieving the International Development Targets*, Strategy Paper, September. London: DFID, http://webarchive.nationalar-chives.gov.uk/+/http://www.dfid.gov.uk/pubs/files/tspgovernment.pdf (accessed 15 February 2013).

DFID (2004) 'Drivers of Change', Public Information Note, September. London: DFID, http://www.gsdrc.org/docs/open/DOC59.pdf (accessed 17 September 2010).

DFID (2009) 'Political Economy Analysis: How To Note', DFID Practice Paper, July. London: DFID, http://www.gsdrc.org/docs/open/PO58.pdf (accessed 11 February 2013).

DFID (2010) 'The Politics of Poverty: Elites, Citizens and States: Findings from Ten Years of DFID-Funded Research on Governance and Fragile States 2001–2010', A Synthesis Paper. London: DFID, http://www.dfid.gov.uk/r4d/PDF/Outputs/FutureState/dfid_Politics_BOOKMARK_SINGLESNEW.pdf (accessed 13 February 2013).

Di John, J. and Putzel, J. (2009) 'Political Settlements', Issues Paper, June. Birmingham: Governance and Social Development Resource Centre (GSDRC).

Djani, L. (2013) 'Reform Movements and Local Politics in Indonesia', PhD Thesis (Murdoch University, Perth, Australia).

Dorn, J. A. (1993) 'Economic Liberty and Democracy in East Asia', *Orbis*, 37 (4): 599–619.

Duncan, A. and Williams, G. (2012) 'Making Development Assistance More Effective Through Using Political-Economy Analysis: What Has Been Done and What Have We Learned?', *Development Policy Review*, 30 (2): 133–48.

Duncan, A., Sharif, I., Landell-Mills, P., Hulme, D. and Roy, J. (2002) 'Bangladesh: Supporting the Drivers of Pro-Poor Change', June. London: DFID (Department for International Development), http://www.gsdrc.org/docs/open/DOC7.pdf (accessed 17 September 2010).

Duncan, R. and McLeod, R. H. (2007) 'The State and the Market in Democratic Indonesia', in R. H. McLeod and A. J. MacIntyre (eds) *Indonesia: Democracy and the Promise of Good Governance* (Singapore: Institute of Southeast Asian Studies (ISEAS)): 73–92.

Easterly, W. (2002) 'The Cartel of Good Intentions: The Problem of Bureaucracy in Foreign Aid', *Journal of Policy Reform*, 5 (4): 223–50.

ECORYS Nederland (2009) 'Strategic Governance and Corruption Analysis: Draft End-of-Project Review'. Rotterdam: ECORYS Nederland.

Eyben, R. (2005) 'Donors' Learning Difficulties: Results, Relationships and Responsibilities', *IDS Bulletin*, 36 (3): 98–107.

Eyben, R. (2007) 'Labelling People for Aid', in J. Moncrieffe and R. Eyben (eds) *The Power of Labelling: How People Are Categorized and Why It Matters* (London: Earthscan): 33–47.

Eyben, R., Guijt, I., Roche, C., Shutt, C. and Whitty, B. (2013) 'The Politics of Evidence: Conference Report', September. Brighton: The Big Push Forward.

Fabella, R. V. (2011) 'Development Thinking and the Rise of Human Agency', in R. V. Fabella, et al. (eds) *Built on Dreams, Grounded in Reality: Economic Policy Reform in the Philippines* (Philippines: The Asia Foundation): 225–51.

Faustino, J. and Fabella, R. V. (2011) 'Development Entrepreneurship', in R. V. Fabella, J. Faustino, M. G. Mirandilla-Santos, P. Catiang, and R. Paras (eds) *Built on Dreams, Grounded in Reality: Economic Policy Reform in the Philippines* (Philippines: The Asia Foundation): 253–71.

Ferguson, J. (1990) *The Anti-Politics Machine: 'Development', Depoliticization and Bureaucratic Power in Lesotho* (Cambridge: Cambridge University Press).

Fine, B. (2003) 'Neither the Washington nor the Post-Washington Consensus: An Introduction', in B. Fine, C. Lapavitsas, and J. Pincus (eds) *Development Policy in the Twenty-First Century: Beyond the Post-Washington Consensus* (London: Routledge): 1–27.

Fine, B. (2006) 'Introduction: The Economics of Development and the Development of Economics', in J. K. Sundaram and B. Fine (eds). *The New Development Economics* (London: Zed): xv–xxi.

Fisher, J. and Marquette, H. (2013) 'Donors Doing Political Economy Analysis™: From Process to Product (and back again?)', Paper presented at the 54th Annual Convention of the International Studies Association, San Francisco, USA, 3–6 April.

Fox, J. (2007) *Accountability Politics: Power and Voice in Rural Mexico* (Oxford: Oxford University Press).

Frey, B. S. (2007) 'Evaluierungen, Evaluierungen … Evaluitis', *Perspektiven der Wirtschaftspolitik*, 8 (3): 207–20.

Friedman, T. L. (1997) 'Quit the Whining: Globalisation Isn't a Choice', *International Herald Tribune*, 9 January. 8.

Fritz, V., Kaiser, K. and Levy, B. (2009) 'Problem-Driven Governance and Political Economy Analysis: Good Practice Framework', September. Washington DC: World Bank, http://siteresources.worldbank.org/EXTPUBLICSECTORAND GOVERNANCE/Resources/PGPEbook121509.pdf (accessed 11 February 2013).

Gamble, A. (1981) *An Introduction to Modern Social and Political Thought* (London: Macmillan).

Gamble, A. (2006) 'The Two Faces of Neo-liberalism', in R. Robison (ed.) *The Neo-Liberal Revolution: Forging the Market State* (Basingstoke: Palgrave Macmillan): 20–38.

Gaventa, J. and McGee, R. (2010) *Citizen Action and National Policy Reform: Making Change Happen* (London and New York: Zed Books).

Gay, R. (1998) 'Rethinking Clientelism: Demands, Discourses and Practices in Contemporary Brazil', *European Review of Latin American and Caribbean Studies*, 65(December): 7–24.

GHK (2011) 'Evaluation of Project Implementation Modalities of the Cities Alliance', Draft Final Report No. J40252307, 4 February. London: GHK.

Gibson, C. C., Andersson, K., Ostrom, E. and Shivakumar, S. (2005) *The Samaritan's Dilemma: The Political Economy of Development Aid* (New York: Oxford University Press).

Gill, S. (1995) 'Globalisation, Market Civilisation and Disciplinary Neoliberalism', *Millennium – Journal of International Studies*, 24 (3): 399–423.

Goetz, A. M. and Jenkins, R. (2005) *Reinventing Accountability: Making Democracy Work for the Poor* (Basingstoke and New York: Palgrave Macmillan).

Grindle, M. S. (1991) 'The New Political Economy: Positive Economics and Negative Politics', in G. M. Meier (ed.) *Politics and Policy Making in Developing Countries: Perspectives on the New Political Economy* (San Francisco: ICS Press): 41–67.

Grindle, M. S. (2004a) *Despite the Odds: The Contentious Politics of Education Reform* (Princeton and Oxford: Princeton University Press).

Grindle, M. S. (2004b) 'Good Enough Governance: Poverty Reduction and Reform in Developing Countries', *Governance*, 17 (4): 525–48.

Grindle, M. S. (2007) 'Good Enough Governance Revisited', *Development Policy Review*, 25 (5): 553–74.

Haas, P. M. (1992) 'Introduction: Epistemic Communities and International Policy Coordination', *International Organization*, 46 (1): 1–35.

Hadiz, V. R. (2003) 'Power and Politics in North Sumatra: The Uncompleted *Reformasi*', in E. Aspinall and G. Fealy (eds) *Local Power and Politics in Indonesia: Decentralisation & Democratisation* (Singapore: Institute of Southeast Asian Studies): 119–31.

Hadiz, V. R. (2004) 'Decentralisation and Democracy in Indonesia: A Critique of Neo-Institutionalist Perspectives', *Development and Change*, 35 (4): 697–718.

Hadiz, V. R. (2007) 'The Localisation of Power in Southeast Asia', *Democratization*, 14 (5): 873–92.

Hadiz, V. R. (2010) *Localising Power in Post-Authoritarian Indonesia: A Southeast Asia Perspective* (Stanford: Stanford University Press).

Hall, P. A. and Taylor, R. C. R. (1996) 'Political Science and the Three New Institutionalisms', *Political Studies*, 44 (5): 936–57.

Hamilton-Hart, N. (2001) 'Anti-Corruption Strategies in Indonesia', *Bulletin of Indonesian Economic Studies*, 37 (1): 65–82.

Hamilton-Hart, N. (2002) *Asian States, Asian Bankers: Central Banking in Southeast Asia* (Ithaca: Cornell University Press).

Harrison, G. (2005) 'The World Bank, Governance and Theories of Political Action in Africa', *British Journal of Politics and International Relations*, 7 (2): 240–60.

Harrison, G. (2006) 'Neo-Liberalism and the Persistence of Clientelism in Africa', in R. Robison (ed.) *The Neo-Liberal Revolution: Forging the Market State* (London: Palgrave Macmillan): 98–113.

Harrison, G. (2010) *Neo-Liberal Africa: The Impact of Global Social Engineering* (London and New York: Zed Books).

Harris, N. (1988) 'New Bourgeoisies', *Journal of Development Studies*, 24 (2): 237–49.

Harriss, J. (2001) *Depoliticizing Development: The World Bank and Social Capital* (London: Anthem).

Harth, K. and Waltmans, J. (2007) 'Behind the Facade: The Informal Reality in Developing Countries', in Effectiveness and Quality Department (DEK) (ed.) *A Rich Menu for the Poor: Food for Thought on Effective Aid Policies* (Essay 3; The Hague: Dutch Ministry of Foreign Affairs): 19–32.

Hatcher, P. (2009) 'The Politics of Entrapment: Parliaments, Governance and Poverty Reduction Strategies', in W. Hout and R. Robison (eds) *Governance and the Depoliticisation of Development* (London: Routledge): 123–36.

Hawes, G. (1987) *The Philippine State and the Marcos Regime: The Politics of Export* (Ithaca: Cornell University Press).

Hay, C. (2002) *Political Analysis: A Critical Introduction* (Basingstoke: Palgrave Macmillan).

Hayek, F. A. (1967) *Studies in Philosophy, Politics and Economics* (London: Routledge and Kegan Paul).

Hewison, K. (1993) 'Of Regimes, States and Pluralities: Thai Politics Enters the 1990s', in K. Hewison, R. Robison, and G. Rodan (eds) *Southeast Asia in the 1990s: Authoritarianism, Capitalism and Democracy* (Sydney: Allen & Unwin): 159–89.

Hewison, K. (2005) 'Neo-Liberalism and Domestic Capital: The Political Outcomes of Economic Crisis in Thailand', *Journal of Development Studies*, 41 (2): 310–30.

Hewison, K. (2006) 'Thailand: Boom, Bust and Recovery', in G. Rodan, K. Hewison, and R. Robison (eds) *The Political Economy of Southeast Asia: Markets, Power and Contestation* (Melbourne: Oxford University Press): 72–106.

Hewitt de Alcántara, C. (1998) 'The Uses and Abuses of the Concept of Governance', *International Social Science Journal*, 50 (155): 105–13.

Hickey, S. (2009) 'Progress Report: The Return of Politics in Development Studies (II): Capturing the Political?', *Progress in Development Studies*, 9 (2): 141–52.

Hickey, S. (2012) 'Turning Governance Upside-down? Insights from the politics of what works', *Third World Quarterly*, 33 (7): 1231–47.

Hidayatulloh, A. (2003) 'Analisa Peran Stakeholders dalam Model Perencanaan MPBM di Kota Mataram', M.Sc Thesis submitted to Magister Perencanaan Kota dan Daerah, Program Pasca Sarjana, Universitas Gadjah Mada.

High-Level Forum on Aid Effectiveness (2005) *Paris Declaration on Aid Effectiveness: Ownership, Harmonisation, Alignment, Results and Mutual Accountability*, Paris, 28 February–2 March. Online, http://www.oecd.org/dac/effectiveness/43911948.pdf (accessed 8 November 2013).

Hill, H. (2000) 'Indonesia to Keep Muddling Through in the Next Few Years', Interview by D. Anggraeni, *Jakarta Post*, 21 December, http://lgtv.thejakartapost.com/index.php/read/news/23760 (accessed 22 February 2013).

Hoffmann, K. (2010) 'The EU in Central Asia: Successful Good Governance Promotion?' *Third World Quarterly* 31(1): 87–103.

Holdstrom, N. and Smith, R. (2000) 'The Necessity of Gangster Capitalism: Primitive Accumulation in Russia and China', *Monthly Review*, 51 (9): 1–7.

Hor Nambora (2009) 'Response to the US Ambassador to Cambodia', *KI-Media: Dedicated to Publishing Sensitive Information About Cambodia* [blog], 4 June, http://ki-media.blogspot.com.au/2009/06/carol-rodley-denounced-corruption-in.html (accessed 1 September 2010).

Hout, W. (2007) *The Politics of Aid Selectivity: Good Governance Criteria in U.S., World Bank and Dutch Foreign Assistance* (London: Routledge).

Hout, W. and Robison, R. (2009) 'Development and the Politics of Governance: Framework for Analysis', in W. Hout and R. Robison (eds) *Governance and the Depoliticisation of Development* (London: Routledge): 1–11.

Houtzager, P. P. (2003) 'Introduction: From Polycentrism to the Polity', in P. P. Houtzager and M. Moore (eds) *Changing Paths: International Development and the New Politics of Inclusion* (Michigan: University of Michigan Press): 1–31.

Houtzager, P. P. and Moore, M. (eds) (2003) *Changing Paths: International Development and the New Politics of Inclusion* (Michigan: University of Michigan Press).

Hudalah, D. and Woltjer, J. (2007) 'Spatial Planning System in Transitional Indonesia', *International Planning Studies*, 12 (3): 291–303.

Hughes, C. (2003) *The Political Economy of Cambodia's Transition, 1991–2001* (London and New York: RoutledgeCurzon).

Hughes, C. (2006) 'The Politics of Gifts: Tradition and Regimentation in Contemporary Cambodia', *Journal of Southeast Asian Studies*, 37 (3): 469–89.

Hughes, C. (2009) *Dependent Communities: Aid and Politics in Cambodia and East Timor* (Ithaca: Cornell Southeast Asia Program Publications).

Human Rights Watch (2006) 'Condemned Communities: Forced Evictions in Jakarta', Volume 18, No. 10 (C), 6 September. New York: Human Rights Watch, http://www.hrw.org/sites/default/files/reports/indonesia0906webw cover.pdf (accessed 1 March 2013).

Hutchcroft, P. D. (1991) 'Oligarchs and Cronies in the Philippine state: The Politics of Patrimonial Plunder', *World Politics*, 43 (3): 414–50.

Hutchcroft, P. D. (1998) *Booty Capitalism: The Politics of Banking in the Philippines* (Ithaca: Cornell University Press).

Hutchison, J. (1997) 'Pressure on Policy in the Philippines', in G. Rodan, K. Hewison, and R. Robison (eds) *The Political Economy of South-East Asia: An Introduction* (Melbourne: Oxford University Press): 64–92.

Hutchison, J. (2007) 'The "Disallowed" Political Participation of Manila's Urban Poor', *Democratization*, 14 (5): 853–72.

Hyden, G. (2008) 'After the Paris Declaration: Taking on the Issue of Power', *Development Policy Review*, 26 (3): 259–74.

IDA (2007) 'IDA's Performance-Based Allocation System: Options for Simplifying the Formula and Reducing Volatility', Washington, DC: IDA, http://documents.worldbank.org/curated/en/2007/02/7411762/idas-performance-based-allocation-system-options-simplifying-formula-reducing-volatility (accessed 9 December 2013).

IDA (2008) 'IDA: The Platform for Achieving Results at the Country Level', IDA 15: Report from the Executive Directors of the International Development Association to the Board of Governors, 28 February. Washington DC: IDA, http://siteresources.worldbank.org/IDA/Resources/Seminar%20PDFs/73449-1172525976405/FinalreportMarch2008.pdf (accessed 9 December 2013).

Imparsial (2009) 'Quo Vadis Satpol PP di Era Reformasi', Press Release, 1 June. Jakarta: *Imparsial*.

Jayasuriya, K. (2005) *Reconstituting the Global Liberal Order: Legitimacy and Regulation* (London: Routledge).

Jayasuriya, K. (2006) 'Economic Constitutionalism, Liberalism and the New Welfare Governance', in R. Robison (ed.) *The Neoliberal Revolution: Forging the Market State* (Basingstoke: Palgrave Macmillan): 234–53.

Jayasuriya, K. and Rodan, G. (2007) 'Beyond Hybrid Regimes: More Participation, Less Contestation in Southeast Asia', *Democratization*, 14 (5): 773–94.

Jessop, B. (2002) *The Future of the Capitalist State* (Cambridge: Polity Press).

Jesudason, J. V. (1996) 'The Syncretic State and the Structuring of Oppositional Politics in Malaysia', in G. Rodan (ed.) *Political Oppositions in Industrialising Asia* (London: Routledge): 128–60.

Joshi, A. and Houtzager, P. P. (2012) 'Widgets of Watchdogs?', *Public Management Review*, 14 (2): 145–62.

Kaffah, E. and Amrulloh, M. A. (eds) (2003) *Fiqh Korupsi: Amanah vs Kekuasaan* (Mataram: Somasi NTB).

Kapstein, E. B. (1999) 'Distributive Justice as an International Public Good: A Historical Perspective', in I. Kaul, I. Grunberg, and M. A. Stern (eds) *Global Public Goods: International Cooperation in the 21st Century* (New York: Oxford University Press): 88–115.

Karaos, A. M. A. (1997) 'Urban Governance and Poverty Alleviation in the Philippines', in E. Porio (ed.) *Urban Governance and Poverty Alleviation in Southeast Asia: Trends and Prospects* (Quezon City: Center for Social Policy and Public Affairs, Ateneo de Manila University): 63–86.

Karaos, A. M. A., Gatpatan, M. V. and Hotz, R. V. (1995) *Making a Difference: NGO and PO Policy Influence in Urban Land Reform Advocacy* (Manila: Institute on Church and Social Issues).

Kaufmann, D., Kraay, A. and Mastruzzi, M. (2007) 'Governance Matters VI: Governance Indicators for 1996–2006', World Bank Policy Research Working Paper No. 4280, July. Washington DC: World Bank, http://papers.ssrn.com/sol3/papers.cfm?abstract_id=999979 (accessed 22 February 2013).

Kessler, C. and Rüland, J. (2008) *Give Jesus a Hand! Charismatic Christians: Populist Religion and Politics in the Philippines* (Quezon City: Ateneo de Manila University Press).

Khalik, A. (2008) 'Informal Sector Helping Indonesia Cope in Global Downturn', *Jakarta Post*, 12 February, http://www.thejakartapost.com/news/2008/12/02/informal-sector-helping-indonesia-cope-global-downturn.html (accessed 1 March 2013).

Khan, M. H. (2005) 'Review of DFID's Governance Target Strategy Paper'. London: School of Oriental and African Studies (SOAS), http://eprints.soas.ac. uk/9955/1/Review_of_Dfid_Governance_TSP.pdf (accessed 15 February 2013).

Khan, M. H. (2010) 'Political Settlements and the Governance of Growth-Enhancing Institutions', July. London: School of Oriental and African Studies (SOAS).

Killick, T. (1998) 'Principals, Agents and the Failings of Conditionality', *Journal of International Development*, 9 (4): 483–95.

Kim, E.K. and Lee, J.E. (2013) 'Busan and Beyond: South Korea and the Transition from Aid Effectiveness to Development Effectiveness', *Journal of International Development*, 25 (6): 787–801.

King, S. J. (2007) 'Sustaining Authoritarianism in the Middle East and North Africa', *Political Science Quarterly*, 122 (3): 433–59.

Koenders, A. G. (2007) 'Democracy and Development: Thinking Forward', presented at 2006–2007 Democracy and Development Lecture Series. Society for International Development (SID), The Hague, 14 September, http://www. government.nl/documents-and-publications/press-releases/2007/09/14/ democracy-and-development-thinking-forward.html (accessed 15 February 2013).

Koenders, A. G. (2008) 'International Cooperation 2.0: Agenda for Modern Poverty Reduction', presented at. University of Amsterdam, 8 November, http://www.minbuza.nl/en/news/speeches-and-articles/2008/11/international-cooperation-2.0.html (accessed 15 February 2013).

Kristiansen, S., Pratikno, S. and Santoso, P. (2004) 'Human Rights and Good Governance in Indonesia: Securing Social and Economic Rights in a Decentralized Government'. Yogyakarta: Agder University College and Fisipol Universitas Gadjah Mada.

Kristof, N. D. and Sanger, D. E. (1999) 'How US Wooed Asia to Let Cash Flow in', *The New York Times*, 16 February, http://www.nytimes.com/library/ world/global/021699global-econ.html (accessed 27 March 2013).

Lancaster, C. (2007) *Foreign Aid: Diplomacy, Development, Domestic Politics* (Chicago: University of Chicago Press).

Lauridsen, L. S. (1998) 'The Financial Crisis in Thailand: Causes, Conduct and Consequences', *World Development*, 26 (8): 1575–91.

Leftwich, A. (2006) 'Drivers of Change: Refining the Analytical Framework – Part 1: Conceptual and Theoretical Issues', *Drivers of Change Studies*, April. London: Department of International Development (DFID), http://www. gsdrc.org/docs/open/DOC103.pdf (accessed 15 February 2013).

Leftwich, A. (2007) 'The Political Approach to Institutional Formation, Maintenance and Change: A Literature Review Essay', Discussion Paper Series No. 14, October. Manchester: Research Programme, Institutions and Pro-Poor Growth (IPPG).

Leftwich, A. (2011) 'Thinking and Working Politically: What Does It Mean? Why Is It Important? And How Do You Do It?', *Policy and Practice for Developmental Leaders, Elites and Coalitions*, Discussion Paper, March. Hawthorn, Australia: Developmental Leadership Program (DLP).

Leftwich, A. (2012) 'Coalitions in the Politics of Development: Findings, Insights and Guidance from the DLP Coalitions Workshop, 15–16 February 2012, Sydney', *Policy and Practice for Developmental Leaders, Elites and Coalitions*, Research and Policy Workshop Report, April. Hawthorn, Australia: Developmental Leadership Program (DLP).

Leftwich, A. and Hogg, S. (2007) 'The Case for Leadership and the Primacy of Politics in Building Effective States, Institutions and Governance for Sustainable Growth and Social Development', *Policy and Practice for Developmental Leaders, Elites and Coalitions*, Background Paper No. 01, November. Hawthorn, Australia: Developmental Leadership Program (DLP), http://www.dlprog.org/ftp/view/Public%20Folder/2%20Background%20Papers/Leaders,%20Elites%20and%20Coalitions.pdf (accessed 13 February 2013).

Leftwich, A. and Hogg, S. (2011) 'The Developmental Leadership Program: Overview and Objectives', *Policy and Practice for Developmental Leaders, Elites and Coalitions*, Background Paper No. 05, February. Hawthorn, Australia: Developmental Leadership Program (DLP), www.dlprog.org.

Leftwich, A. and Wheeler, C. (2011) 'Politics, Leadership and Coalitions in Development: Findings, Insights and Guidance from the DLP's First Research and Policy Workshop, Frankfurt 10–11 March 2011', *Policy and Practice for Developmental Leaders, Elites and Coalitions*, A Research and Policy Workshop Report, June. Hawthorn, Australia: Developmental Leadership Program (DLP), www.dlprog.org.

Levi, M. (2006) 'Why We Need a New Theory of Government', *Perspectives on Politics*, 4 (1): 5–19.

Leys, C. (1996) *The Rise and Fall of Development Theory* (Bloomington: Indiana University Press; Nairobi: EAEP).

Lindsey, T. (2000) 'Black Letter, Black Market and Bad Faith: Corruption and the Failure of Law Reform', in C. Manning and P. van Diermen (eds) *Indonesia in Transition: Social Aspects of Reformasi and Crisis* (Singapore: Institute of Southeast Asian Studies): 278–92.

Lyne de Ver, H. and Kennedy, F. (2011) 'An Analysis of Leadership Development Programmes Working in the Context of Development', *Policy and Practice for Developmental Leaders, Elites and Coalitions*, Research Paper 11, February. Hawthorn, Australia: Developmental Leadership Program (DLP), http://www.dlprog.org/ftp/view/Public%20Folder/1%20Research%20Papers/An%20Analysis%20of%20Leadership%20Development%20Programmes.pdf (accessed 8 March 2013).

Marcelino, E. (2005) 'Advocacy for the Pasig River Communities', *Policy Advocacy: Experiences and Lessons from the Philippines* (Quezon City: Institute for Popular Democracy): 107–26.

Massey, S. and May, R. (2006) 'Commentary: The Crisis in Chad', *African Affairs*, 105 (420): 443–49.

Maxwell, S. (2005) 'The Washington Consensus Is Dead! Long Live the Meta-Narrative!', Working Paper 243, January. London: Overseas Development Institute, http://dspace.cigilibrary.org/jspui/bitstream/123456789/22891/1/The%20Washington%20Consensus%20is%20Dead%20Long%20Live%20the%20Meta%20Narrative.pdf?1 (accessed 15 February 2013).

McCourt, W. (2003) 'Political Commitment to Reform: Civil Service Reform in Swaziland', *World Development*, 31 (6): 1015–31.

McLeod, R. H. (2005) 'The Struggle to Regain Effective Government Under Democracy in Indonesia', *Bulletin of Indonesian Economic Studies*, 41 (3): 367–86.

Melo, M. A., Ng'ethe, N. and Manor, J. (2012) *Against the Odds: Politicians, Institutions and the Struggle against Poverty* (London: Hurst & Company).

Minister for Development Cooperation (1998) '*Brief Met Beleidsvoornemens Inzake Toepassing Van Criteria Op Het Vlak Van De Structurele Bilaterale Ontwikkelingshulp* (Letter to Parliament on the Application of Criteria Related to Structural Bilateral Development Assistance)', Second Chamber, 1998–99 Session, 26200V No. 8. The Hague: Dutch Government.

Minister for Development Cooperation (2003) '*Aan Elkaar Verplicht: Ontwikkelingssamenwerking Op Weg Naar 2015* (Mutual Interests, Mutual Responsibilities: Dutch Development Cooperation En Route to 2015)', Second Chamber, 2003–4 Session, 29234 No. 1, 3 October. The Hague: Dutch Government, http://www.eerstekamer.nl/id/vhyxhwt7jvy4/document_extern/w29234b1/f=/w29234b1.pdf (accessed 20 February 2013).

Minister for Development Cooperation (2007) 'Our Common Concern: Investing in Development in a Changing World', Policy Note Dutch Development Cooperation 2007–2011, October. The Hague: Ministry of Foreign Affairs (Development Cooperation), http://www.minbuza.nl/binaries/content/assets/minbuza/de/import/de/das_ministerium/entwicklungszusammenarbeit/our-common-concern.pdf (accessed 20 February 2013).

Minister for European Affairs and International Cooperation (2011) '*Focusbrief Ontwikkelingssamenwerking* (Focus Letter to Parliament on Development Cooperation)', 18 March, http://www.rijksoverheid.nl/bestanden/documenten-en-publicaties/kamerstukken/2011/03/18/aanbiedingsbrief-focusbrief-ontwikkelingssamenwerking/os-focusbrief.pdf (accessed 12 April 2011).

Ministry of Foreign Affairs (2008) 'Framework for Strategic Governance and Corruption Analysis (SGACA): Designing Strategic Responses towards Good Governance', October. The Hague: Ministry of Foreign Affairs, http://capacity4dev.ec.europa.eu/governance/document/framework-strategic-governance-and-corruption-analysis-sgaca-designing-strategic-responses-(accessed 11 March 2013).

Moertopo, A. (1973) *The Acceleration and Modernisation of 25 Years Development* (Jakarta: Centre for Strategic and International Studies).

Montes, M. F. (1989) 'Philippine Structural Adjustments, 1970–1987', in M. F. Montes and H. Sakai (eds) *Philippine Macroeconomic Perspective: Developments and Policies* (Tokyo: Institute of Developing Economies): 45–90.

Moore, M. (2001) 'Political Underdevelopment: What Causes Bad Governance', *Public Management Review*, 3 (3): 385–418.

Moore, M. and Putzel, J. (1999) 'Thinking Strategically About Politics and Poverty', IDS Working Paper 101. Brighton, UK: Institute of Development Studies (IDS), http://www.ids.ac.uk/files/Wp101.pdf (accessed 15 February 2013).

Mouffe, C. (1993) *The Return of the Political* (London: Verso).

Mulholland, M. and Burke, J. (2012) 'UK to halt India aid and focus on trade', *The Guardian*, 10 November, http://www.theguardian.com/global-development/2012/nov/09/uk-india-aid-trade (assessed 15 March 2013).

Murphy, D. and Anana, T. (2004) 'Pasig River Rehabilitation Program'. Habitat International Coalition, http://www.hic-net.org/document.php?pid=2668 (accessed 4 November 2013).

Natsios, A. (2010) 'The Clash of the Counter-Bureaucracy and Development', *Center for Global Development Essay*, July. Washington DC: Center for Global Development (CGD), http://www.cgdev.org/files/1424271_file_Natsios_Counterbureaucracy.pdf (accessed 15 February 2013).

North, D. C. (1994) 'Economic Performance through Time', *American Economic Review*, 84 (3): 359–68.

North, D. C. (1995) 'The New Institutional Economics and Third World Development', in H. John, J. Hunter, and C. M. Lewis (eds) *The New Institutional Economics and Third World Development* (London: Routledge): 17–26.

Olson, M. (1965) *The Logic of Collective Action: Public Goods and the Theory of Groups* (Harvard: Harvard University Press).

Olson, M. (1982) *The Rise and Decline of Nations: Economic Growth, Stagflation and Structural Rigidities* (New Haven: Yale University Press).

Ostrovsky, A. (2003) 'Old Style Rituals Mark New Sign of Capitalist Russia', *Financial Times*, 14 July. 3.

Ostrovsky, A. (2004) 'Chubais Defends Sell-Offs as Saviour of Russian Economy', *Financial Times*, 16 April. 3.

Oversloot, H. (2006) 'Neo-Liberalism in the Russian Federation', in R. Robison (ed.) *The Neo-Liberal Revolution: Forging the Market State* (London: Palgrave Macmillan): 58–78.

Paris, R. (2004) *At War's End: Building Peace after Civil Conflict* (Cambridge: Cambridge University Press).

Parks, T. and Cole, W. (2010) 'Political Settlements: Implications for International Development Policy and Practice', Occasional Paper No. 2, July. The Asia Foundation.

Pasuk Phongpaichit and Baker, C. J. (2004) *Thaksin: The Business of Politics in Thailand* (Bangkok: Silkworm Books).

PBSP (2007) *Keeping in Step: Forging Partnerships, Changing Lives* (Manila: Philippine Business for Social Progress).

PICUM (2010) 'PICUM's Main Concerns about the Fundamental Rights of Undocumented Migrants in Europe 2010', October. Brussels: PICUM, http://picum.org/picum.org/uploads/publication/Annual%20Concerns%202010%20EN.pdf (accessed 4 November 2013).

Pinches, M. D. (2010) 'The Making of Middle Class Civil Society in the Philippines', in Y. Kasuya and N. G. Quimpo (eds) *The Politics of Change in the Philippines* (Manila: Anvil Publishing, Inc.): 284–312.

Porio, E., Crisol, C. S., Magno, N. F., Cid, D. and Paul, E. N. (2004) 'The Community Mortgage Programme: An Innovative Social Housing Programme in the Philippines and Its Outcomes', in D. Mitlin and

D. Satterthwaite (eds) *Empowering Squatter Citizen: Local Government, Civil Society and Urban Poverty Reduction* (London: Earthscan): 54–81.

Poulantzas, N. A. (1978) *State, Power, Socialism* (London: NLB).

Racelis, M. (2005) 'Begging, Requesting, Demanding, Negotiating: Moving Towards Urban Poor Partnerships in Governance', in N. Hamdi and J. Handal (eds) *Urban Futures: Economic Growth and Poverty Reduction* (Rugby, UK: ITDG Publishing): 69–88.

Rapaczynski, A. (1996) 'The Roles of the State and the Market in Establishing Property Rights', *Journal of Economic Perspectives*, 10 (2): 87–103.

Reno, W. S. K. (1997) 'African Weak States and Commercial Alliances', *African Affairs*, 96 (383): 165–85.

Resosudarmo, B. P., Yamauchi, C. and Effendi, T. (2009) 'Rural-Urban Migration in Indonesia: Survey Design and Implementation', CEPR Discussion Paper No. DP630, December. Canberra: Centre for Economic Policy Research, Research School of Economics: Australian National University, http://cbe.anu.edu.au/research/papers/ceprdpapers/DP630.pdf (accessed 8 March 2013).

RGC (2009) 'National Strategic Development Plan: Update 2009–2013', November. Phnom Penh: Royal Government of Cambodia, http://www. gafspfund.org/sites/gafspfund.org/files/Documents/Cambodia_6_of_16_ STRATEGY_National_Strategic_%20Development_Plan.NSDP__0.pdf (accessed 27 February 2013).

RGC (2010) *Chbap Stey Pi Kar Prachang Ampoeu Puk Roluey (Law on Anti-Corruption): Draft Submitted to National Assembly.*

Robison, R. (1986) *Indonesia: The Rise of Capital* (Sydney: Allen & Unwin).

Robison, R. (1988) 'Authoritarian States, Capital-Owning Classes, and the Politics of Newly Industrializing Countries: The Case of Indonesia', *World Politics*, 41 (1): 52–74.

Robison, R. (1996) 'The Politics of "Asian Values"', *The Pacific Review*, 9 (3): 309–27.

Robison, R. (2006) 'Indonesia: Crisis, Oligarchy, and Reform', in G. Rodan, K. Hewison, and R. Robison (eds) *The Political Economy of Southeast Asia: Markets, Power and Contestation* (Melbourne: Oxford University Press): 109–36.

Robison, R. (2009) 'Strange Bedfellows: Political Alliances in the Making of Neo-Liberal Governance', in W. Hout and R. Robison (eds) *Governance and the Depoliticisation of Development* (London: Routledge): 15–28.

Robison, R. (2012) 'Interpreting the Politics of Southeast Asia: Debates in Parallel Universes', in R. Robison (ed.) *Routledge Handbook of Southeast Asian Politics* (Oxon and New York: Routledge): 5–22.

Robison, R. and Hadiz, V. R. (2004) *Reorganising Power in Indonesia: The Politics of Oligarchy in an Age of Markets* (London: Routledge).

Robison, R., Wilson, I. D. and Meliala, A. (2008) '"Governing the Ungovernable": Dealing with the Rise of Informal Security in Indonesia', Asia Research Centre Policy Brief No.1, June. Perth, Australia: Asia Research Centre, Murdoch University, http://wwwarc.murdoch.edu.au/publications/ wp/pb1.pdf (accessed 8 March 2013).

Rodan, G. (1996) 'The Internationalization of Ideological Conflict: Asia's New Significance', *The Pacific Review*, 9 (3): 328–51.

Rodan, G. (2006a) 'International Capital, Singapore's State Companies and Security', in G. Rodan and K. Hewison (eds) *Neoliberalism and Conflict in Asia After 9/11* (London: Routledge).

Rodan, G. (2006b) 'Neo-Liberalism and Transparency: Political Versus Economic Liberalism', in R. Robison (ed.) *The Neo-Liberal Revolution: Forging the Market State* (London: Palgrave Macmillan): 197–215.

Rodan, G. and Hughes, C. (2012) 'Ideological Coalitions and the International Promotion of Social Accountability: The Philippines and Cambodia Compared', *International Studies Quarterly*, 56 (2): 367–80.

Rodan, G. and Hughes, C. (2014) *The Politics of Accountability in Southeast Asia: The Dominance of Moral Ideologies* (Oxford: Oxford University Press).

Rosser, A. J. (2009) 'Rebuilding Governance in Failed States: The Case of Timor Leste', in W. Hout and R. Robison (eds) *Governance and the Depoliticisation of Development* (London: Routledge): 169–82.

Rotberg, R. I. (2012) *Transformative Political Leadership: Making a Difference in the Developing World* (Chicago and London: University of Chicago Press).

Rukmana, D. (2007) 'Urban Planning and the Informal Sector in Developing Countries', *Planetizen*. 7 May, http://www.planetizen.com/node/24329 (accessed 20 November 2013).

Rukmana, D. (2009) 'A City without Social Justice', *Inside Indonesia*, 98 (October–December).

Ryan, M., Richardson, S. and Voutier, P. (2012) *Business in Development Study 2012* (Accenture), http://www.accenture.com/us-en/Pages/insight-business-development-study-2012.aspx (accessed 2 December 2013).

Ryder, H. (2013) 'The rise of development effectiveness', *The Guardian*, 13 March, http://www.theguardian.com/global-development-professionals-network/2013/mar/13/development-effectiveness-dfid-aid-india/print (accessed 9 November 2013).

Sabarini, P. (2009) 'In Search of More Space for Street Vendors', *Jakarta Post*, 12 February, http://www.thejakartapost.com/news/2009/02/12/in-search-more-space-street-vendors.html (accessed 8 March 2013).

Sachs, J. (1992) 'What Is to Be Done', *The Economist*, 13 January, http://www.economist.com/node/13002085 (accessed 22 February 2013).

Samdech Hun Sen, S. P. M., Head of the Royal Government of Cambodia (1997) 'Main Points on the Establishment of a Neutral Political Environment and Security for Elections', *Gathering with Civil Servants, the Armed Forces, Governors and Deputy Governors from Some Provinces and Townships* (Preah Sihanouk City Theater Hall, Sihanouk Ville).

Sangmpam, S. N. (2007) 'Politics Rules: The False Primacy of Institutions in Developing Countries', *Political Studies*, 55 (1): 201–24.

Schakel, L., Hout, W., Slob, A. and Smith, D. (2010) 'The Use of Political Economy Assessment Instruments in the Governance Sphere', *ECORYS Research Programme Report*. Rotterdam: ECORYS Nederland.

Scott, J. and Wilkinson, R. (2011) 'The Poverty of the Doha Round and the Least Developed Countries', *Third World Quarterly*, 32 (4): 611–27.

Secretary of State for International Development (1997) 'Eliminating World Poverty: A Challenge for the 21st Century', White Paper on International Development, Cm 3789, November. London: Department for International Development (DFID), http://webarchive.nationalarchives.gov.uk/+/http://www.dfid.gov.uk/policieandpriorities/files/whitepaper1997.pdf (accessed 20 February 2013).

SEESAC (2006) *Evaluation of the EU SALW Assistance to the Kingdom of Cambodia* (Belgrade: SEESAC).

Setiyono, B. and McLeod, R. (2010) 'Civil Society Organisations' Contribution to the Anti-Corruption Movement in Indonesia', *Bulletin of Indonesia Economic Studies*, 46(3): 347–370.

Shatkin, G. (2007) *Collective Action and Urban Poverty Alleviation: Community Organizations and the Struggle for Shelter in Manila* (London: Ashgate).

Silverman, B. and Yanowitch, M. (1997) *New Rich, New Poor, New Russia: Winners and Losers on the Russian Road to Capitalism* (New York: M. E. Sharpe, Inc.).

Simpson, G. R. (2008) 'How Lobbyists Kept the Risky Loans Coming: Sub Prime Lenders Donated Millions to Discourage a Legislative Crackdown', *Wall Street Journal/The Australian*, 2 January. 15.

Social Alert International (2005) 'Organising Informal Economy Workers in Indonesia', Research Report. Brussels: Social Alert International, http://wiego.org/publications/organising-informal-economy-workers-indonesia (accessed 8 March 2013).

STAR Kampuchea Organization (2007) 'Landlessness and Land Conflict in Cambodia'. Phnom Penh: International Land Coalition, http://www.landcoalition.org/sites/default/files/legacy/legacypdf/07_r%5Bt_land_cambodia.pdf?q=pdf/07_r[t_land_cambodia.pdf (accessed 3 August 2010).

Steinberg, F. (2010) 'Preparing the Metro Manila Urban Services for the Poor Project', Technical Assistance Completion Report PPTA 4616-PH. Manila: Asian Development Bank (ADB), http://www.adb.org/sites/default/files/projdocs/2010/38398-01-phi-tcr.pdf (accessed 13 February 2013).

Storey, D. (2013) 'Troubled Waters: Rehabilitating the Pasig River, the Philippines', in Lee Poh Onn (ed.) *Water Issues in Southeast Asia: Present Trends and Future Directions* (Singapore: Institute of Southeast Asian Studies): 174–211.

Sumner, A. (2012) 'Where Do the Poor Live?', *World Development*, 40 (5): 865–877.

Sumner, A. and Mallett, R. (2013) *The Future of Foreign Aid: Development Cooperation and the New Geography of Poverty* (Basingstoke: Palgrave Macmillan).

Suparno, R. (2007) 'RI Too Democratic to Progress', *The Jakarta Post*, 8 June. 4.

Tangri, R. and Mwenda, A. M. (2001) 'Corruption and Cronyism in Uganda's Privatisation in the 1990s', *African Affairs*, 100 (398): 117–33

Tangri, R. and Mwenda, A. M. (2003) 'Military Corruption and Ugandan Politics since the Late 1990s', *Review of African Political Economy*, 98 (30): 539–52.

Thornton, N. and Cox, M. (2005) 'Review of the Uptake of the Drivers of Change Approach', *Report for the Department for International Development (DFID)*, June. London: Agulhas Development Consultants.

Tolentino, V. B. J. (2010) 'From Analysis to Implementation: The Practice of Political Economy Approaches to Economic Reform', Occasional Paper No. 3, September. San Francisco: The Asia Foundation, http://asiafoundation. org/resources/pdfs/OccasionalPaperNo3lowres.pdf (accessed 11 February 2013).

Toye, J. (1987) *Dilemmas of Development* (Oxford: Blackwell).

Transparency International (2009) 'Corruption Perceptions Index 2009'. Berlin: Transparency International, http://archive.transparency.org/policy_ research/surveys_indices/cpi/2009/cpi_2009_table (accessed 3 April 2013).

UBS (2006) 'Indonesia Connections', 23 May. Jakarta: UBS.

Un, K. and Hughes, C. (2011) 'The Political Economy of "Good Governance" Reform', in K. Un and C. Hughes (eds) *Cambodia's Economic Transformation* (Copenhagen: Nordic Institute of Asian Studies (NIAS) Press): 199–218.

UN (2002) 'Outcome of the International Conference on Financing for Development: Report of the Secretary General', August, http://dac-cess-dds-ny.un.org/doc/UNDOC/GEN/N02/535/43/PDF/N0253543. pdf?OpenElement (accessed 20 November 2013).

UNDP (2012) 'Key Facts about Poverty Reduction in Cambodia', *UNDP in Cambodia* [webpage], http://www.undp.org/content/cambodia/en/home/ ourwork/povertyreduction/in_depth.html (accessed 26 November 2013).

UN-Habitat (2003) 'The Challenge of Slums: Global Report on Human Settlements 2003'. London: Earthscan Publications Ltd., http://www.unhabitat.org/ pmss/listItemDetails.aspx?publicationID=1156 (accessed 1 March 2013).

Unsworth, S. (2005) 'Focusing Aid on Good Governance: Can Foreign Aid Instruments Be Used to Enhance "Good Governance" in Recipient Countries?', GEG Working Paper 2005/18, 23 February. Oxford: Global Economic Governance Programme (GEG), http://www.globaleconomic governance.org/wp-content/uploads/Unsworth%20-%20Focusing% 20Aid%20on%20Good%20Governance.pdf (accessed 7 October 2011).

Unsworth, S. (2009) 'What's Politics Got to Do with It?: Why Donors Find It so Hard to Come to Terms with Politics, and Why This Matters', *Journal of International Development*, 21 (6): 883–94.

van de Walle, N. (2001) *African Economies and the Politics of Permanent Crisis, 1979–1999* (Cambridge: Cambridge University Press).

Van der Veen, A. M. (2011) *Ideas, Interests and Foreign Aid* (Cambridge: Cambridge University Press).

van Gastel, J. and Nuijten, M. (2005) 'The Genealogy of the "Good Governance" and "Ownership" Agenda at the Dutch Ministry of Development Cooperation', in D. Mosse and D. J. Lewis (eds) *The Aid Effect: Giving and Governing in International Development* (London: Pluto Press).

Volkov, V. (2002) *Violent Entrepreneurs: The Use of Force in the Making of Russian Capitalism* (Ithaca: Cornell University Press).

Wade, R. (1998) 'The Asian Debt and Development Crisis of 1997–? Causes and Consequences', *World Development*, 26 (8): 1535–53.

Waltmans, J. (2008) 'Behind the Façade: From Analysis to Action', in Effectiveness and Quality Department (DEK) (ed.) *A Rich Menu for the Poor: Food for Thought on Effective Aid Policies* (Essay 15; The Hague: Dutch Ministry of Foreign Affairs): 175–88.

Warrener, D. (2004) 'The Drivers of Change Approach', Synthesis Paper 3, November. London: Overseas Development Institute, http://www.odi.org.uk/sites/odi.org.uk/files/odi-assets/publications-opinion-files/3721.pdf (accessed 13 February 2013).

Watts, J. (2006) 'The Savannah Comes to Beijing as China Hosts its New Empire', *The Guardian*, 4 November. 24.

Weyland, K. (2003) 'Neopopulism and Neoliberalism in Latin America: How Much Affinity?', *Third World Quarterly*, 24 (6): 1095–115

Whitfield, L. and Therkildsen, O. (2011) 'What Drives States to Support the Development of Productive Sectors? Strategies Ruling Elites Pursue for Political Survival and Their Policy Implications', DIIS Working Paper No 2011:15. Copenhagen: Danish Institute for International Studies (DIIS).

Williams, D. (2008) *The World Bank and Social Transformation in International Politics: Liberalism, Governance and Sovereignty* (London and New York: Routledge).

Williams, D. and Young, T. (1994) 'Governance, the World Bank and Liberal Theory', *Political Studies*, 42 (1): 84–100.

Williams, G., Duncan, A., Landell-Mills, P. and Unsworth, S. (2011) 'Politics and Growth', *Development Policy Review*, 29 (S1): S29–S55.

Williamson, J. (1994) 'In Search of a Manual for Technopols', in J. Williamson (ed.) *The Political Economy of Policy Reform* (Washington DC: Institute for International Economics): 11–28.

Williamson, O. E. (1987) *The Economic Institutions of Capitalism* (New York: The Free Press).

Wilson, I. D. (2006) 'Continuity and Change: The Changing Contours of Organized Violence in Post-New Order Indonesia', *Critical Asian Studies*, 38 (2): 265–97.

Wilson, I. D., Djani, L. and Masduki, T. (2009) '"Governing Favours": An Investigation of Accountability Mechanisms in Local Government Budget Allocation in Indonesia', Australia Indonesia Governance Research Partnership Policy Brief No.8. Canberra: Australian National University, http://www.aigrp.anu.edu.au/docs/projects/1035/Wilson_Masduki_brief.pdf (accessed 5 November 2010).

Wilson, R. (2002) 'Promoting Good Governance: Some Lessons from History and Recent Experience', presented at Politics and Governance, Overseas Development Institute. London, 12 June, http://www.odi.org.uk/events/2132-promoting-good-governance-lessons#audio/video (accessed 15 February 2013).

Wisnu, A. (2009) 'Relocation Remains a Painful Topic for Vendors', *Jakarta Post*, 10 March, http://www.thejakartapost.com/news/2009/10/03/relocation-remains-a-painful-topic-vendors.html (accessed 8 March 2013).

World Bank (1981) 'Accelerated Development in Sub-Saharan Africa: An Agenda for Action', No. 14030. Washington DC: World Bank, http://www-

wds.worldbank.org/external/default/WDSContentServer/IW3P/IB/2000/04/
13/000178830_98101911444774/Rendered/PDF/multi_page.pdf (accessed
27 March 2013).

World Bank (1991) 'Managing Development: The Governance Dimension',
Discussion Paper No. 34899, 29 August. Washington DC: World Bank,
http://www-wds.worldbank.org/external/default/WDSContentServer/
WDSP/IB/2006/03/07/000090341_20060307104630/Rendered/PDF/34899.
pdf (accessed 22 February 2013).

World Bank (1997) *The State in a Changing World: World Development Report
1997* (New York: Oxford University Press).

World Bank (2001) *Attacking Poverty: World Development Report 2000/2001*
(Oxford and New York: Oxford University Press).

World Bank (2002a) *Building Institutions for Markets: World Development Report
2002.* (Oxford and New York: Oxford University Press).

World Bank (2002b) 'World Bank Group Work in Low-Income Countries under
Stress: A Task Force Report', September. Washington DC: World Bank, http://
siteresources.worldbank.org/INTLICUS/Resources/388758-1094226297907/
Task_Force_Report.pdf (accessed 22 February 2013).

World Bank (2003) 'Combating Corruption in Indonesia: Enhancing
Accountability for Development', October. Jakarta: World Bank, http://
siteresources.worldbank.org/INTINDONESIA/Resources/Publication/03-
Publication/Combating+Corruption+in+Indonesia-Oct15.pdf (accessed 22
February 2013).

World Bank (2004) *Making Services Work for the Poor: World Development Report
2004* (Oxford and New York: Oxford University Press).

World Bank (2005) *Economic Growth in the 1990s: Learning from a Decade of
Reform* (Washington DC: World Bank).

World Bank (2006) 'Making the New Indonesia Work for the Poor',
Indonesia Poverty Analysis Program (INDOPOV), November. Jakarta:
World Bank, http://siteresources.worldbank.org/INTINDONESIA/
Resources/226271-1168333550999/PovertyAssessment.pdf (accessed 14
November 2010).

World Bank (2007a) 'Sharing Growth: Equity and Development in Cambodia',
Equity Report No. 39089–KH, 4 June. Phnom Penh: World Bank – East Asia
and the Pacific Region, http://siteresources.worldbank.org/INTCAMBODIA/
Resources/293755-1181597206916/E&D_Full-Report.pdf (accessed 3 August
2010).

World Bank (2007b) *The State in a Changing World: World Development Report
1997.* (Oxford and New York: Oxford University Press).

World Bank (2008a) 'The Political Economy of Policy Reform: Issues
and Implications for Policy Dialogue and Development Operations',
Report No. 44288-GLB, 10 November. Washington DC: World Bank,
http://siteresources.worldbank.org/EXTSOCIALDEV/Resources/Political_
Economy_of_Policy_Reform.pdf (accessed 18 February 2013).

World Bank (2008b) 'Project Appraisal Document on a Proposed Grant in the
Amount of SDR 12.8 Million (US$20 Million Equivalent) to the Kingdom
of Cambodia for a Demand for Good Governance Project', 23 October.

Washington DC: World Bank, Sustainable Development Department, East Asia and Pacific Region, http://www-wds.worldbank.org/external/default/ WDSContentServer/WDSP/IB/2008/11/17/000333038_20081117234338/ Rendered/PDF/423660PAD0P1011LY10IDA1R20081029711.pdf (accessed 27 February 2013).

World Bank (2008c) 'World Bank Helps Cambodia to Strengthen the Demand for Good Governance', Press Release No. 2008/164/EAP, 3 December. Washington DC: World Bank, http://web.worldbank.org/WBSITE/EXTERNAL/PROJECTS/ 0,,contentMDK:21998041~menuPK:64282138~pagePK:41367~piPK:279616~ theSitePK:40941,00.html (accessed 1 September 2010).

World Bank (2013a) 'Cambodia Overview', *World Bank* [webpage], http://www. worldbank.org/en/country/cambodia/overview (accessed 14 February 2013).

World Bank (2013b) 'What Is Demand for Good Governance' [webpage], http://go.worldbank.org/7OGYRXOG50 (accessed 4 November 2013).

Wright, E. O. (2000) 'Working-Class Power, Capitalist-Class Interests, and Class Compromise', *American Journal of Sociology*, 105 (4): 957–1002.

Index

Printed and bound in the United States of America